The Biblical
Path to
Psychological
Maturity

The Biblical Path to Psychological Maturity

Psychological Insights into the Weekly Torah Readings

Vivian B. Skolnick, Ph.D.

KODESH PRESS

ISBN: 978-0692024539

Published by
Kodesh Press L.L.C.
www.kodeshpress.com
kodeshpress@gmail.com
New York, NY

Dedication

THIS BOOK IS dedicated primarily to my beloved husband, who has encouraged and sponsored my education and who labored diligently in editing this book. Many of the discussions presented here have been between us and our family at the Shabbat table. My children, Dr. Blair Skolnick and his wife, Andy Tuttie Skolnick; their children, Noam and Ditza Skolnick; and my daughter Sarelle Skolnick Weiner and her husband, Rabbi Heschel Weiner; and their children Yosef and his wife Bryna; as well as Elazar, Yaakov, Doni, Shevi, Yedidya, and Yonah, have all been participants in the "think tank" that has helped me formulate my ideas. Although our family is religiously observant and uses recognized traditional sources, our discussions were always diverse and lively because of the perspective lent by my professional and academic insights. I am indebted to my family for being such a source of light and love for me.

Vivian B. Skolnick, Ph.D.
Chicago, 2008

ACKNOWLEDGMENTS

ONE OF THE main adventures of psychoanalysis is to go back and see where you came from, and how those early experiences have impacted your past and present life. This same discovery process helped shape the creation of this book. The love of being Jewish was instilled in me by my parents, Rabbi Morris and Pauline Blair. My husband, Dr. Irving Skolnick, guided me in writing this book and spent countless hours editing the manuscript. Thank you to Dr. Gordon Maguire, my mentor and psychoanalyst for spending so much time helping me edit my life, and whose wisdom and educational devotion prepared me to reach my life's goals. Many thanks also go to my son-in-law Rabbi Heschel Weiner who not only checked the Judaic sources for my ideas, but who inspired my creative thinking in interpreting the text. Ana Benson has proven to be far more than a computer maven and transcriber of the text; she found and executed the graphics thereby enhancing this volume's innovative structure. My Bible classes with Rabbi Dr. Abe Lipshitz for over twenty years added immeasurably to my understanding of the Bible by adding another level of discourse to my education. To my patients, thank you for teaching me that reaching maturity opens the path for greater spiritual fulfillment on various levels and directions.

All your contributions have helped me realize my dreams.

V. B. Skolnick

TABLE OF CONTENTS

GENESIS

EXODUS

LEVITICUS

NUMBERS

Deuteronomy

INTRODUCTION

THERE IS PRECEDENT within Jewish tradition for psychoanalytic interpretation of the Torah, although not identified as such. The Midrash during the Greco-Roman period already provides metaphoric insights into human behavior which border on psychological analysis. In Kabbalistic circles, and subsequently with the rise of the Hasidic movement in the late 18th century, Bible commentators were delving into the hidden emotional, unconscious implications of the Torah text. This search for the hidden internal landscape of human emotions is especially evident in Rabbinic interpretation of Biblical dreams. It is therefore not surprising that among the books found in Dr. Sigmund Freud's library was the Babylonian Talmud *Berachot*, in which a complete chapter is devoted to the subject of dreams. Apparently, Freud was aware of Rabbinic discussions on this subject. Although psychoanalysis is one of the newer disciplines discussing Biblical themes, insights of a psychological genre, often referred to as human nature, have been with us from time immemorial.

Beginning with the book of Genesis, one finds fertile ground for psychoanalytic explication. Adam and Eve are portrayed as beset by unrestrained narcissistic desires typical of young children. Matters of good and evil are a foreign realm to them; they are being driven by the need for instant gratification. In succeeding chapters, from that of Cain and Abel, through the lives of the patriarchs and matriarchs in the book of Genesis, and through the life of Moses concluding with the book of Deuteronomy, we see a pattern of gradual development of human potential moving toward maturity. In many respects this parallels the developmental stages of a child's growth pattern leading toward adulthood.

Whether for an individual or for a people, the process of growth toward maturity is the true test of progress and stability.

The presenting issues that bring clients into my consulting room, very often are caused by difficulties with their parental or spousal relationships, not unlike the stories in the Bible. For example, marital issues which arise because of the husband's inability to commit to the role of husband/father are often disguised as devotion to one's profession or to other priorities. How is this different from what appears to be a deteriorating relationship between Abraham and Sarah, caused by Abraham's willingness to sacrifice Sarah's only son Isaac? Albeit a supreme example of faith and commitment to God, it was nevertheless, according to some commentators, the immediate cause of Sarah's death. Isaac's favoritism toward his wayward son Esau was not merely a product of physical blindness, but a form of transference, wherein Isaac, who was passive by nature, wishes to become identified with the aggressiveness of his son, Esau. Eating the venison brought by Esau can be viewed as a metaphor for Isaac's internalizing this desired aggressive character trait. The enduring enmity between Jacob and Esau may stem from a breakdown of communication between Isaac and Rebeccah over raising their children, as each favored a different son. The character transformation of Jacob into becoming Israel, represented more than a change of identity, but was a result of Jacob's working through his psychological struggles caused by being a twin and being raised in a conflicted household. Jacob, like his grandfather Abraham, and later his son Joseph, was destined to leave his family for new surroundings in order to realize his potential. These departures were not only physical separations, but set the stage for the patriarchs to shed their former identities by going through a difficult process of individuation leading to future greatness. Conversely, Isaac, who never left his family of origin to explore new vistas, remained in a state of arrested development symbolized by only being able to rediscover the wells dug by his father Abraham, rather than becoming a distinctive creative personality in his own right. No one personified dramatic change as much as Joseph, whose dreams and remarkable skill at dream interpretation propelled him to become second only to the Pharaoh of Egypt. He became a role model for Freud in probing the depths of the unconscious that lay hidden in the symbolism of dreams.

The entire saga of Moses, described in the last four books of the Torah, tracks the developmental growth of a hesitant stammering shepherd who felt inadequate and afraid to lead, into becoming one of history's greatest leaders. His transformation from being a violence-prone Egyptian prince into becoming Israel's greatest prophet is a paradigm for the evolution of his people who shed their slave mentality and prevailed over many challenges prior to their entry into the Promised Land. Bible commentators indirectly address some of these psychological issues; they do so by means of the scholarly art of exegesis/hermeneutics (*drash*), grammatical nuances and contextual clues. However, contemporary readers not versed in these scholarly techniques may miss the emotional impact of events experienced by Biblical personalities which have relevance to their own lives. The fact is that the penetrating wisdom inherent in the Torah transcends time and space. My task as a psychoanalyst is to target and capture the impact of those feelings, to interpret them from a psychological perspective, and to label them with modern psychological terminology. This new language unlike the traditional universe of discourse in vogue in Biblical times, helps make the Torah more vital and accessible to our more psychologically oriented readers.

As an observant woman psychoanalyst—an anomaly to both my Orthodox friends and psychoanalyst colleagues—I have attempted to apply the fruits of my professional training in revealing the psycho-dynamic underpinnings of Biblical events and figures. The synagogue's cycle of weekly Sabbath Torah readings provides a practical framework for the examination of the psychological issues experienced by Torah figures. These weekly readings begin with the book of Genesis on the Festival of *Simhat Torah* (usually in early October), and the cycle is concluded a year later on this

Festival. An additional incentive in adopting this sequential framework is to enable families to discuss the ramifications of the weekly Torah portion at their Sabbath tables as I was privileged to do with my family. In so doing, I shall attempt to show that the Torah encapsulates a developmental growth pattern akin to human development. As the Torah concludes with the death of Moses, we witness the transformation of a small nomadic Abrahamic clan into becoming the Children of Israel. From a psychoanalytic perspective this is a journey from childhood narcissism to adult spiritual maturity. In my professional practice I have seen similar transformations; secular patients after successful analysis find a need for some type of spiritual fulfillment to fill the former emptiness in their lives. The enduring appeal of the Bible is precisely its humaneness as it embraces the issues that relate to the lives of its readers. By analyzing the Biblical text from a psychological/psychoanalytic perspective, it becomes more than an historical account of compelling religious interest, but a modern instructive guide into the dynamics of human behavior.

Contrary to detractors who feel that psychoanalysis, a purely secular science, is incompatible with a faith-based religion, I have found these disparate fields to be complementary and mutually instructive. No better metaphor for this accommodation is the story of Zusia, the Hasidic master, who was reputed to have carried two reminder notes, one in each pocket. On one was written the Hebrew phrase, *anochi afar ve-efer*, "I am but dust and ashes." On the other was written, *bishvili nivra ha-olam*, "the world was created for me." Whenever Zusia was consumed with self-importance, he would reach for the note with the admonition, "remember you are but dust and ashes." When he found himself overcome by depression, he would reach for the note reminding him of his noble spiritual origins and would be comforted. These two notes in the parable represent two different states of being—helplessness versus a sense of power. These are the essential psychological states the Israelites experienced during their forty year journey in the wilderness. Moses served as both leader and psychological mentor in guiding his people from a state of helplessness and dependence to gaining a sense of power and independence. On a psychological level this represents an advance from an infantile narcissistic state ("And she [Eve] saw that it [the forbidden fruit] was a delight to the eyes...") to one of adult responsibility ("we shall do and we shall hearken") the hallmark of maturity. In this process, Moses exemplifies behavior change by undergoing his own personal journey from early family separation to reaching the peak of adult spiritual fulfillment. The Torah depicts this personal and collective journey in factual physical terms, but their gradual psychological development is implicit throughout the narrative, if we but probe into finding the hidden emotional connections. Hopefully, finding these psychological connections will reward the reader with a better understanding of his/her own struggle between the physical and spiritual as did the Biblical personalities in the five books of the Torah.

Vivian B. Skolnick, Ph.D.

EDITOR'S NOTE

FOREMOST IN EDITING is my desire to facilitate understanding of this work by a diverse readership representing various backgrounds and religious beliefs. This desire generated my idea of providing a Summary of the weekly Torah portions read sequentially in the synagogue during Sabbath services. Those not accustomed to this weekly format of readings will find these Summaries helpful in deriving an organized concise overview of the entire Torah during the course of a year's readings.

FORMAT: Each *Parshah* (weekly Torah portion) is captioned by its transliterated Hebrew name and positioned on the left-hand page, followed by the topic heading and summary of the *Parshah*. The author's commentary begins on the right-hand matching page with her topic heading.

TRANSLATION of the Hebrew Biblical text adopted in this work is based on *The Pentateuch and Haftorahs* by J. H. Hertz. This translation preserves the time-honored distinct flavor of the English language associated with Bible study.

TRANSLITERATION of Hebrew words is a complex task owing to the absence of certain Hebrew letters in the English alphabet. The transliteration system adopted here is an eclectic one, geared to easing pronunciation of Hebrew by English speakers, rather than following any of the more complex systems extant in scholarly circles. The transliterated Hebrew words are italicized in the commentary and underlined in the summary of the *Parshiyot*.

QUOTATIONS cited from the weekly Torah readings are annotated.

REFERENCES to various books, articles and authors are not annotated, but can be found in the Bibliography at the end of this work.

GLOSSARY of recurring Hebrew terms is provided as an additional aid to understanding the Hebrew texts.

I. H. Skolnick, D.H.L.
Chicago

THE BOOK OF GENESIS

"In the beginning God created the heaven and the earth"
— *Genesis* 1:1

Bereshith
Genesis 1:1—6:8
Creation of the World

*T*he origin of the universe is described as beginning with G-d, the Creator, executing a series of creations over a span of six days. The pinnacle of these creative acts is the beginning of the human race, with the creation of Adam on the sixth day. G-d rests on the seventh day, which is sanctified as a day of rest. Adam is joined by Eve, who is created from his side, and becomes his help- mate. They are placed in the Garden of Eden where they meet up with the sly serpent. The serpent seduces Eve into eating from the forbidden fruit of the Tree of Knowledge. Eve proceeds to give the forbidden fruit to Adam who also indulges. This "original sin" warrants G-d's severe punishment to each of the sinners. Adam and Eve are then expelled from the garden. Cain and Abel are the first offspring of the union of Adam and Eve. When G-d favors the offering of Abel over that of his brother, Cain, retaliates by killing his brother, Abel. Cain is punished by being banished from G-d's presence. Eve gives birth to another son, Seth, who fathers many descendants. There follows a listing of Cain's offspring, culminating in the birth of Noah, who fathers three sons: Shem, Ham and Japheth. This extensive genealogy stemming from Adam and Eve is followed by G-d's ominous observation that this proliferated mankind is totally consumed with evil. The Parshah concludes with G-d's decision to wipe humankind off the face of the earth, yet declaring that "Noah found grace in the eyes of the Lord."

Creation:
A Metaphor for Human Potential

The mystery of G-d's creation of the universe, with its untold secrets governing the physical world, is also a metaphor for the unfolding development of mankind. While we will never know exactly how the world was created, it is sufficient for the Torah to let us know that it was G-d who did it; it was done in six days/stages, moving from the simple to the complex. The design of the creation was according to the Torah, for the purpose of bringing order out of chaos. G-d's instrument in carrying out this purpose on earth is man, i.e., Adam. The creation story provides mankind with an introduction and a baseline for the basic principle of bringing order out of chaos in human affairs and in the human psyche.

Part of the design of maintaining order on earth is already stated in the first chapter, where man is instructed to have dominion over the animal kingdom (Gen. 1:26). The fact that animals were also created on the sixth day (same as Adam) lends credence to the idea of drawing certain parallels between them. Animals are similar to humans in having genetically based instincts and impulses. Animals mature by giving full range to their impulses in order to survive. Humans are, however, endowed with superior powers of intelligence and speech. These powers enable them to learn how to control their cauldron of intense animalistic impulses and desires.

Both animals and humans are unfinished creations, but in different ways. Man has to finish himself through internal maturation, whereas animals evolve through adapting themselves to different external physical conditions. The degree to which man succeeds in this internal struggle represents his growth and development toward maturity. Freud described this maturation process in psychoanalytic terminology, "where the id was, there ego shall be." In other words, a person's self, "ego," is defined by one's ability to control the "id," our innate uncontrolled feelings and desires. This is the human challenge to bring order out of chaos. When translating Freud's insight of human behavior into the creation story, G-d's mandate for man to have "dominion" over the animal kingdom entails a twofold process, external and internal. Dominion means more than exerting outer physical control; it is a psychological metaphor for the human struggle to control our internal animalistic cravings and impulses. The tension of this internal psychological struggle is dramatized at the very beginning of creation.

In chapter two, the scene shifts to Adam and Eve to show how this internal struggle operates on the human level as a result of their interaction with the serpent. The immediate appearance of the serpent in the Garden of Eden is the Torah's prescient way of letting us know that our animal impulses (id) exist within us from our very beginning. Adam and Eve, the first humans, are like infants with underdeveloped psyches in adult bodies, who are subject to a multitude of animalistic desires where there is no distinction between good, evil, greed, and gratitude. Enter the serpent, representing the animalistic forces of unrestrained desire, blurring the parameters between good and evil. The primeval chaos is now reenacted on the human level, as the serpent confuses Adam and Eve by reversing roles, and by exploiting Eve's childish need for instant gratification. In this chaotic scenario, it is the animal, the serpent, who is endowed with the human gifts of intelligence and speech, while Eve is reduced to behaving like an indecisive animal along with Adam her equally gullible helpmate. Their childlike behavior is put on display in the opening pastoral scene in the Garden of Eden, where Adam and Eve are forbidden to eat the fruit from the Tree of Knowledge of Good and Evil. The obvious question arises, why is such a basic knowledge of life considered a forbidden object? The answer lies in the Torah's presenting, at the very outset of creation, psychological insights into the vagaries of human behavior.

One of these insights is the basic idea that in order to have successful relationships there must be boundaries. This is true in the physical realm of human relationships as well as in the spiritual realm in relating to G-d. In order for humans to develop and grow toward maturity they have to learn what are the appropriate boundaries for safety and structure. This was provided for Adam and Eve in the idyllic surroundings of the Garden of Eden, with the exclusion of the Tree of Knowledge. This tree becomes the test case for Adam and Eve to learn this object lesson about observing boundaries. When boundaries break down, whether externally in relating to others (Adam and Eve to G-d) or internally in controlling one's desires (eating the forbidden fruit), then mankind is at risk. Then mankind returns to the state of internal chaos represented by the serpent, a descent into the lower animal kingdom.

Another insight into human behavior occurs when the serpent promises Adam and Eve that they can be like G-d by eating from the Tree of Knowledge. This is a metaphor for the illusion that mortals can be all-knowing. It also provides an early psychological lesson for mankind which is to learn to curb grandiose feelings of narcissism and omnipotence. This childish narcissism can be overcome eventually when one learns how to adapt to the various developmental stages in growing up toward maturity. The Tree of Knowledge metaphor represents the first parental lesson that Adam and Eve would have to learn, that if you are not ready to accept the boundaries of good and evil set by Me (G-d), then you cannot have freedom and the Garden of Eden. You must then struggle to work through the hardships of life East of Eden in the real world in order to develop the ability and maturity to tame the cauldron of impulses and desires inside of you.

The psychodrama that is played out between the key figures in the Garden of Eden is being replayed today in the psychologists' consulting rooms. Several of the psychological issues touched upon in the creation story occur in my practice. Whereas the modern context of these disorders has changed, the underlying issues are nevertheless still present. For example, the forbidden fruit and Eve's irresistible desire to indulge are the psychological ingredients that can develop into eating disorders identified today as bulimia, anorexia and weight issues. After Adam and Eve eat of the forbidden fruit of the Tree of Knowledge the Torah states, "And the eyes of them both were opened and they knew they were naked, and they sewed fig leaves together and made themselves girdles… and the man and his wife hid themselves from the Lord…" (Gen. 3:7-8). Inherent in their behavior are the beginning signs of sexual difficulties between the genders as well as fear of exposure (nakedness).

One of the main presenting issues in my treating married couples is this issue of exposure, revealing oneself to his/her partner. This exposure is much more intrusive than the physical nakedness referred to in our text. They fear that they will be prematurely exposed and stand naked and defenseless before the therapist. They are therefore quite guarded about revealing themselves. Once, however, this wall of resistance is overcome, the chances of resolving differences between them are greatly enhanced. In such cases I have found that sexual differences are openly discussed for the first time in their marriage. It is this fear of exposure, revealing who we really are, which is bound to cause relationship difficulties. Whether with Adam and Eve or with our modern couple, it is the act of exposure, "baring one's soul," that launches the therapeutic process. Successful treatment is achieved through openness leading to the goal of adult maturity. It is also through the safety of the therapeutic frame that enables the patient to overcome the fear of one's internal impulses, and the fear of presenting oneself as a whole person to the world.

The etiology of the psychological disorders discussed above as well as the "original sin" committed by Adam and Eve is therefore basically the same. It derives from Freud's insight about the maturation process which is predicated on building a sense of self (ego). Without a structured ego, one is left with a feeling of emptiness. This condition may derive from a variety of personal problems such as lack of love in growing up, feelings of inferiority or other inadequacies. When this condition persists, the tendency is to fill the void artificially with food, drugs, sex, Internet, etc. Without a developed ego and evolving maturity, there is no barrier against the pull of these impulses. Adam and Eve sheltered from the real world had not developed internal identities and therefore easily succumbed to their id impulses shared with their animal neighbors.

We can now understand why when G-d created man He did not say that "it was good" as was the case with the other days of creation. The intention of the Torah is to show that man, like the universe, needs to go through stages as in the process of creation by creating himself into a complete, ethical and responsible person. One has to leave the Garden of Eden, i.e., your mother's arms, where everything is provided for you as long as you stay little and immature *a la* Adam and Eve. When the child completes the stages of growth leading to maturity and responsibility, only then can one truly declare, "It was good." It is only when Adam and Eve are forced to live in the real world East of Eden that they begin to experience the daily problems of life and coalesce into a family. In this way they learn to develop themselves and become whole internally as well as externally. These are the same dynamics of treatment that require time-consuming working through the issues of life in order to see positive results.

As we begin the book of Genesis we are embarking on a psychological as well as physical journey in time and space. Judging from the ancestors of mankind, we are at the earliest infantile stage of human development. As we track the Biblical narrative recorded in the weekly Torah readings, we find ourselves treading on the path that helped define the lives of the patriarchs, matriarchs and the heroic figure of Moses, prophet and teacher. How they coped with the many challenges they faced can serve as an example in ordering our own lives. By penetrating into the emotional and psychological aspects of their lives, we are privy to better understanding of our own lives and of choosing the appropriate path leading to greater maturity and spiritual fulfillment.

Noah

Genesis 6:9-11:32

The Flood

*I*n view of the total corruption and violence of the descendants of Adam and Eve, with the notable exception of G-d-fearing Noah, G-d decides to bring a flood to destroy mankind. Noah is instructed to build an ark to enable his family and specific animals to escape the flood. The build up of the flood is described in stages, until it finally recedes allowing Noah, et al, to leave the ark. G-d gives Noah the sign of the rainbow as a covenant never again to flood the world. Noah plants a vineyard and becomes intoxicated from its fruit. Ham his son is cursed by Noah when it is discovered that he did not show filial respect during Noah's lapse. The Torah then lists the genealogy of the various nations who descended from Noah's three sons; Shem, Ham and Japheth. Mankind is then concentrated in Babel and speaking a similar language. They, however, used this unity to build a tower for self aggrandizement as opposed to acknowledging G-d's omnipotence. They are punished by being dispersed and by confounding their language. The Parshah concludes by tracing the ten generations from Noah to Abram, who is destined to become the founder of the Hebrew people.

The Maturation Process: Bringing Order out of Chaos

At the end of the previous *Parshah*, G-d states, "I will blot out man whom I have created.... And Noah found favor in the eyes of G-d" (Gen. 6:7-8). There was something special that singled out Noah and made him worthy of saving. A key character trait in describing Noah is the Hebrew term *tamim*, variably translated as a "whole/complete person." From a psychological perspective, a person of this type would merit the term "mature," a trait associated with being grown up and responsible. Noah, unlike the first set of parents, Adam and Eve, is characterized as "whole," i.e., mature, "who walks with G-d" (Gen. 6:1). In this early stage of mankind's development, there is recognition that its behavior is infantile, full of "evil inclination," impulse ridden with an inner psychic landscape of chaos.

In Freud's view, the early infant is mostly driven by the "id," the untamed impulses and urgent needs. The process of civilizing the child starts with a model of good parenting, by satisfying the child's needs within certain boundaries and by teaching the child to channel the chaos of the id into structured ego. As the child begins to take charge of his own internal psyche, he is then capable of dealing appropriately with his external environment. There is then less need for the parent to be the sole determiner of right and wrong, good and evil and bringing order out of chaos. So it is with this *Parshah* and subsequent ones as well, where we see that mankind is in its most infantile psychological state, unable to provide structure for itself and necessitating that G-d takes over parental duties by creating structure for safety, growth and ethical stability. It is into this deteriorated milieu that G-d intervenes by selecting Noah, representing the mature responsible adult, to carry out His plan of again bringing order and structure out of chaos. What better way of symbolizing this concept than building a structure, i.e., an ark? The specific instructions for building the Ark provided a structure for safety. Without this structure, mankind would perish.

In the flood story, G-d further demonstrates that the process of bringing mankind out of its infantilized state to one of order and regeneration is a gradual and deliberate one. It is accomplished in stages (as in creation), which is represented metaphorically in the number forty. Whereas in psychological literature, the child's growth into maturity is accomplished in stages, in the Biblical idiom it is referred to in days or years, *a la* the days of creation. We see this symbolically in the forty days and forty nights of rain to cover and wash away the evil. "And it came to pass at the end of forty days, that Noah opened the window" (Gen. 8:6), a symbolic act that life could begin again.

This theme of gradual psychic development is played out frequently in the Bible, sometimes accompanied by the number "forty," as in years of Israel's travels in the desert. This gave the Israelites the necessary time to overcome their Egyptian slave mentality. The giving of Torah to Moses in "forty days" is recognition of the time-consuming nature of acquiring wisdom and behavioral change. In fact the number "forty" is regarded in *Ethics of the Fathers* (5:24), as the age of understanding, presumably by then one has overcome the major problems associated with growth and maturity. We see from these examples that growth is not a one-time happening, but a process occasionally represented by the number forty that continues throughout life. This process enables man to take over responsibility for himself and move from a primitive chaotic state toward a more structured ordered psyche. Under these promising developments, there is no longer a need for total destruction to do away with evil, e.g., the flood. There is a gradual reliance that mankind will use its G-d-given free will guided by the Torah, to create a world of order and structure thereby relieving G-d of His parental duties to do this for them.

In this sense, the Creation and Flood stories are really one. The main theme continues to be the bringing of order out of chaos which is an important part of the maturation process. G-d, the Supreme Parent, chooses Noah who embodies the trait of maturity, *tamim*, and charges him with the task of building an ark to save mankind. This three-tiered structure which we are told took 120 years to build (multiple of 40), was divided in such a way as to accommodate all its inhabitants and preserve internal order. As with Adam and Eve who were expelled from their birthplace, so too with Noah and his family, they resurface on distant Mt. Ararat where they start life anew.

The psychoanalytic model of the mind also consists of a three-tiered structure: id, ego and superego (conscience). The ascent of humanity is measured in the degree of growth from curbing one's inner impulses to developing a sense of self, and a moral conscience to discern between right and wrong. Noah serves as such a model for the primitive generations of his era. This entails external physical movement which is symbolic of movement from dependence to independence in the hope that mankind would grow and mature. This lesson in appropriate parenting and movement toward independence will continue to be replayed in the lives of the patriarchs, and later in the lives of the Israelites under the leadership of Moses.

Lech Lecha
Genesis 12:1-17:27
History of the Patriarchs

G-d speaks to Abram and informs him that he must leave (Lech Lecha) his familiar surroundings and journey to an unknown destination where he is destined to found a great nation. Due to a famine, Abram and his attractive wife Sarai are detoured into Egypt where she is taken captive into Pharaoh's home. After the clarification of a misunderstanding whether Sarai was Abram's sister or wife, she was released. As they continue their journey together with Abram's nephew, Lot, and his family, it becomes necessary for them to part company. Lot opts to settle in the wicked city of Sodom. When a war between local chieftains results in Lot's capture, Abram succeeds in rescuing him, yet refuses to accept any of the spoils offered to him by the king of Sodom. In a mystical rite, G-d promises Abram that he will father a great nation, however his people will have to undergo four hundred years of slavery. In the end they will inherit the land occupied by the Canaanite nations. This scene is the basis for the eternal Covenant between G-d and the descendants of Abram which is symbolized by the rite of male circumcision. To this end, G-d promises Abram age one hundred, and Sarai age ninety that they will have a son in fulfillment of the Covenant. To commemorate their new life changing mission, G-d changes their Hebrew names from Abram to Abraham and from Sarai to Sarah.

"The Deeds of the Patriarchs are an Omen for their Children"
— *Bereshith Rabbah* 48

The above quoted Midrashic statement is often used to show the profound influence the example of the patriarchs had upon succeeding generations. Upon deeper analysis, it is also a psychological insight into gaining independence from parents in order to establish one's own identity. Although we know that the most profound influence on one's life are the values and ideals of parents, one of the signs of approaching maturity is the ability of the child to question those values and ideals. This does not mean that in questioning we give up those values, because after questioning we often become more committed to them by internalizing and making them our own. When there is, however, deviation or innovation, and embarking on a newly inspired road after a period of questioning and sorting, a conflict sometimes arises between the new challenging outlook in contrast to the security of the old.

In the case of Abraham, there are two conflicting views in the Midrash as to why he broke with the old, and became the founder of the new Hebrew nation. One view is that Abraham, in surveying the universe, arrives at monotheism through his own intelligence in opposition to the ancient idolatrous beliefs of his father, Terah. In so doing, Abraham rejects his father and all that he stood for in order to move in a new direction. Another view depicts his father, Terah, as an innovator, for he had the courage and ability to separate from the great Sumerian civilization of Ur and start a new life for his family in Haran. Terah therefore served as a positive role model for Abraham to enable his son to separate from him, not only physically but also intellectually.

From a psychological perspective this latter view would help explain why Abraham was not afraid to heed G-d's call to leave Haran, since his father before him had set such an example by leaving his birthplace. G-d's call to Abraham, *Lech Lecha* (which literally means "go for you," for your own growth and exploration), is that now is the time for you to leave your father's house, so that you can develop your own identity, sense of leadership, maturity, values and ideals without deposing your father. You now have the opportunity to rely on your own inner resources, rather than continue the stance of childhood dependency on external resources.

Ana-Maria Rizzuto, a psychoanalyst who researched the development of faith and the G-d image from childhood to adulthood, states that adolescence is the most important stage, because the adolescent begins to form images and ideas about G-d that are independent of the introjected parental image. To be able to think and question, allows the adolescent to filter parental values through his own psyche which then become his own, even though they may or may not be identical to the parental values. The ability to think, question and process in an environment of freedom, allows the adolescent to feel separate enough that whatever conclusions he draws, they are his, not a childish repetition of someone else's ideals. When an adolescent or adult has to live up to someone else's ideals which are not congruent with his own, there is often a sense of shame.

This is the dilemma which Abraham faces, that there is this lack of congruence between his own well thought out ideals and reality and those of his father, Terah. To follow something that made no sense to him, and that he could not believe in, would leave Abraham with a sense of shame. In following his own ideals, Abraham demonstrated mature judgment and enhanced self-esteem. This could be the meaning of the above Midrashic statement, *ma'aseh avot siman la-banim*. Parental influence is a *siman*, a sign, an omen or model, but it is up to the individual to move beyond the sign toward maturity. In so doing, *Lech Lecha* means using parental values creatively by being able to differentiate from them in forming one's own personal identity.

The true test of maturity is one's ability to harmonize these two polarities—parental/dependence and individual/independence. One of the main manifestations of Abraham's greatness lies in his ability to balance these opposing forces. G-d's directive *Lech Lecha* spurred Abraham to begin this journey even at the advanced age of seventy-five. This patriarchal sign became the unconscious call for his descendants to continue on this journey toward psychological maturity. The psychological wisdom of the above Midrashic statement has been proven to me repeatedly during treatment in both its positive and negative forms. The sins of the parents are frequently visited upon their children in spite of all conscious efforts to prevent this from happening. For example, a young woman complains of being in a troubled marriage not unlike that of her parents. Somehow the familiar conditions which she experienced as a child, albeit negative, are unconsciously repeated in spite of all conscious efforts to prevent them from happening. On the other hand, a patient reared in a loving, caring family, despite current spousal difficulties has a much better prognosis in treatment because of a feeling of trust engendered by a caring therapist and parental moral support. This pattern of generational behavioral repetition is confirmed in the recent research of H. Fainberg, *The Telescoping of Generations*. This "modern" research has its generational repetition theory already validated by the generations of the patriarchs and matriarchs. It really begins to take shape with the appearance of Abraham, whose towering innovative character made it possible for him to break with the past, and become the founding patriarch of a new nation.

Vayera
Genesis 18:1-22:24
The Akeidah: Trial of Abraham

*F*ollowing his circumcision, Abraham is visited by three men/ angels. One of them announces that the aged Sarah will deliver a son within the year. G-d informs Abraham of His intention to destroy the wicked city of Sodom. Abraham bargains with G-d to spare the righteous among them. When none can be found, the cities of Sodom and Gomorrah are destroyed. Lot and his daughters survive. Thinking all mankind was destroyed, the two daughters of Lot conspire to have relations with their father, from which eventually, derive the nations of Ammon and Moab. A similar episode to that of Pharaoh's earlier abduction of Sarah occurs with Avimelech, king of Gerar, with the same result. Sarah is freed. As promised by the man/angel, Sarah gives birth to a son, Isaac. Sarah and Abraham's concubine, Hagar, have a strained relationship resulting in Hagar and son, Ishmael, being evicted into the arid wilderness. An angel rescues Ishmael, and Hagar is promised that Ishmael will father a great nation. Abraham's faith is being tested when he is asked by G-d to sacrifice his son, Isaac. He passes the test, as an angel intervenes at the last minute to rescue Isaac. The Parshah concludes with a genealogy of Abraham's extended family, culminating in the birth of Rebeccah.

Oedipal Problems
in Abraham's Family

The *Akeidah* (binding/sacrifice of Isaac) is usually looked upon as a supreme example of martyrdom and faith. However, the emotional toll this event must have taken on the family members is equally compelling. The Midrash tells us (see Rashi to Gen. 23:2) that when Sarah was apprised of the impending sacrifice of her beloved son, Isaac, "her soul departed," i.e., she died instantly. This is an instance when the Midrash is not weaving a metaphor or parable, but is conveying a sensitive down-to-earth reaction of a despondent mother. Sarah, during all the childless years of her marriage to Abraham, was a loyal partner with her husband, in caring for wayfarers, i.e., *hachnasat orchim*, accompanying him to depraved Egypt and helping convert strangers to the One G-d. For all of these years, Abraham had the full attention of his beloved Sarah. Can one imagine Sarah's joy in finding herself pregnant and giving birth to a son at age ninety after all those demeaning barren years? Her view of herself as a complete woman had been badly damaged, for which the miraculous birth of Isaac was a deep psychological restitution. For Abraham, however, it is more of a religious experience in fulfillment of G-d's promise to multiply his seed. He already experienced fatherhood through his son, Ishmael, so the birth of Isaac did not have the same emotional, psychological importance as it did for Sarah. For her, Isaac becomes the focus of her life, usurping this position which Abraham had enjoyed all of their married life. There is a psychological basis for conjecturing that Abraham now harbors conflicting feelings in relation to his wife Sarah and the newborn son Isaac. This may have stirred up competitive oedipal feelings in Abraham toward his growing son who is dominating Sarah's life. Along with being submissive to G-d's will, Abraham is harboring an unconscious anger at Isaac for being deposed by him in Sarah's eyes. This complex emotional background sets the stage years later for the traumatic *Akeidah*.

One may question Abraham's lack of protest at G-d's request to sacrifice Isaac, whereas he was most vocal in protesting the destruction of the evildoers in Sodom and Gomorrah, "Wilt Thou sweep away the righteous with the wicked?" (Gen. 18:23). When bearing in mind, however, the emotional climate of the family, caused in part by Abraham's anger with Sarah's over attachment to Isaac, his silence in protesting the *Akeidah* becomes more comprehensible. Apparently, Abraham is thinking only of his special relationship to G-d, and not of the impact the *Akeidah* would have upon his wife and son. The Midrash while not expressing itself in psychological terms, seems to empathize with Sarah's sense of double loss, that of her husband's commitment to her, and the loss of the son who represents her immortality. To continue her life under these circumstances proves unbearable. Her disillusionment and disappointment after a lifelong partnership of working with Abraham must have led to deep depression as all the life is drained out of her ("her soul departed"). It is interesting to note that after the *Akeidah* there is no more reported discourse in the text between Sarah and Abraham. Isaac is so traumatized that he lives the rest of his life as a psychologically wounded individual who never attains any particular distinction. This kind of extreme trauma perpetrated by a parent leaves the child with a lifelong feeling of shame and guilt, "If my parent does this to me, there must be something wrong with me." Though a person may cover this shame and inferiority with some measure of success or skill in some areas, deep down there is a feeling of an ineradicable flaw. So Isaac may have moved on with his life and married and had children, but he would never have a sense of feeling authentically successful.

Kohut, the noted psychoanalyst describes this type of personality, as one which may create a compliant, false sense of self as a mask to cover a deeper sense of inferiority and being flawed. Isaac may have developed this psychological condition due to what is currently described as post traumatic stress disorder (PTSD). The *Akeidah*, therefore, not only presents a theological stress point, but from a psychological perspective it will have serious repercussions later in Isaac's family relationships.

Hayei Sarah
Genesis 23:1-25:18
Death and Burial of Sarah

Upon the death of his wife, Sarah, at age 127, Abraham purchases a large family plot in Hebron from Ephron, the Hittite. To avoid having his son, Isaac, marry a local Canaanite woman, Abraham dispatches his faithful servant, Eliezer, to Haran to seek a wife from among his family members. Eliezer happens to meet Rebeccah at a well, where she shows great concern for this stranger and his thirsty camels. Taking this as a Divine sign, Eliezer is taken by Rebeccah to meet her father, Laban. Realizing that they are kinsmen and with Rebeccah's consent, Eliezer returns to his master, Abraham, to introduce Rebeccah to her intended groom, Isaac. The Parshah concludes by recording the death of Abraham at age 175, followed by a genealogy of his descendants, especially, of his son Ishmael, who dies at age 137.

The Mourning
Process and Therapy

This *Parshah* has a beginning and ending theme of mourning and loss. It opens with a statement that Sarah died in Hebron at age of one hundred and twenty-seven and that Abraham immediately attends to her burial by acquiring a grave-site. The *Parshah* ends by relating that "Abraham expired and died in good old age, an old man, and full of years and was gathered to his people" (Gen. 25:8). Rashi, a primary commentator on the Torah, uncharacteristically makes little comment on the many obvious redundancies in the description of Abraham's death, yet is expansive in commenting on the fewer redundancies in the description of Sarah's death. "And Sarah lived one hundred years and twenty years and seven years; the years of Sarah's life" (Gen. 23:1). Moreover, the Torah states that "Abraham came to eulogize Sarah and [then] to weep for her" (Gen. 23:2), a reversal of the usual sequence when hearing about the death of one's life partner.

The delay in Abraham's ability to weep for Sarah may be symptomatic of what psychologists refer to as denial, often accompanied by feelings of guilt. Considering that Abraham was very upset with Sarah's insistence on dispatching Hagar and his son, Ishmael, "And the thing was evil in the eyes of Abraham because of his son [Ishmael]" (Gen. 21:11), it is most surprising that Abraham did not react this way, when told to sacrifice his son, Isaac. As noted above, he willingly complied without challenging the efficacy of G-d's request. Sarah may have viewed her husband's lack of protest on behalf of Isaac, yet doing so for

43

Ishmael as abandonment of his responsibilities as husband and father. Consequently, Abraham had good reason to feel guilty and unable to weep upon hearing about Sarah's death. Rashi, attentive to the nuances in the deaths of Sarah and Abraham, therefore found the former more significant and deserving of elaboration than the latter.

In the Torah's description of Abraham's mourning experience, there are certain parallels with patients who are undergoing treatment. In fact, therapy and traditional Jewish mourning practices share some of the same procedures. For example, in therapy the patient begins speaking first (not the therapist), and begins to eulogize the losses in his/her life, the unfulfilled dreams, and the loss of relationships. In so doing, the patient is able to cry and mourn those losses. According to Jewish tradition, the mourner is also first to initiate the conversation with the comforters by recounting memories of the deceased. The therapist, in listening, acknowledges the losses, bringing some measure of solace to the patient, in much the same way as the comforters by listening bring solace to the mourner. Social chit-chat is discouraged in both settings in order to focus on discussing the losses and the need to remove the outer social masks and deal with feelings. The mourner takes off the social mask in not wearing makeup, wearing a ripped garment, and not being concerned with putting on a "good face" for the public. Similarly, the patient "lets his/her hair down" during treatment, by exposing one's true inner self. Both therapy and mourning are a time-consuming process engaged in over a lengthy period of time. Traditional Jewish mourning is divided into phases of up to a year, lessening in intensity over time, as in therapy, where the positive effects of treatment are gradually internalized by the patient. Once the treatment/mourning process is completed one can get on with the business of life.

In our *Parshah* we see how unresolved family issues can lead to stunted depressed lives. Sarah according to the Midrash eventually retreated into a solitary world in Kiryat-arba/Hebron where she died. All of these unresolved issues weigh heavily on Abraham in his latter years, and are transmitted to his son, Isaac, resulting in thwarting the full development of his personality. Abraham's delayed tears are, however, stimulated by talking, reminiscing and eulogizing, which cause him to regain the feelings of grievous loss of his beloved wife, Sarah. Only then is he able to cry.

Toldot
Genesis 25:19-28:9
Generations

A fter a period of barrenness and a difficult delivery Rebeccah gives birth to twins, Esau and Jacob. They are total opposites, not only in physical appearance but in character. Esau, the ravenous hunter is even willing to sell his birthright to Jacob for a mere bowl of lentil soup. During a famine, Isaac travels to the land of the Philistines where there is a replay with the king, Avimelech, regarding his "sister" Rebeccah, as happened with his father, Abraham. Isaac re-digs wells that were dug by his father, Abraham, and were filled by the Philistines, and he prospers greatly.

A plot unfolds whereby Rebeccah, aware of the aged, blind Isaac's intention of blessing his favorite son, Esau, schemes to substitute her favorite, the more worthy son, Jacob, in order for him to receive his father's coveted blessing. The plot unravels as Esau appears for his father's blessing only to find that his brother, Jacob, has usurped his favored position. Nevertheless, Isaac also blesses Esau, but the enmity between the two brothers increases to the point whereby Rebeccah advises Jacob to flee for his life to her brother, Laban. This is also in keeping with Isaac's wishes that Jacob find a wife there among his kinsmen rather than among the Canaanite daughters. Esau also fulfills his father's wishes by marrying Mahalath, daughter of Ishmael, son of Abraham.

Being True to Oneself

The title of this *Parshah*, which is *Toldot* ("Generations"), is saying volumes in typical Biblical understatement with the following opening words, "And these are the generations of Isaac, son of Abraham: Abraham begot Isaac" (Gen. 25:19). This obvious redundancy is the Torah's terse way of drawing attention to the powerful psychological impact Abraham had upon his son, Isaac both positively and negatively. It is also a subtle statement that family issues get transmitted from generation to generation. It causes us to step back and recognize the Torah's psychological perceptiveness in gauging the power of the parental dynamic in character formation of the family. The only missing factor is the absence of psychological language which did not exist at that time. Today all mental health professionals recognize in treating physical and emotional problems, the importance of taking a family history. We see G-d as it were, in the role of psychoanalyst, taking notes and recording the development of the patriarchal family as it proceeds in various directions. This record is not above showing shortcomings in this family, so one gets the feeling that these are real people in a real world. Each person has some difficulty to overcome, and each *Parshah* is like watching a therapy session unfold, as we track the expansion of egos of individuals and groups. G-d gives the interpretation of people and events in oblique fashion so we are not always sure of its meaning. That makes it all the more intriguing and the subject of so many differing opinions. However, one thing is clear in this *Parshah*, and that is the powerful influence of Abraham in shaping the destiny of the patriarchal family, especially on his son, Isaac.

Having been so traumatized by his father Abraham during the ordeal of the *Akeidah*, Isaac develops a sense of himself as dependent and helpless. He is from that time on, in a stage of arrested development, lacking a firm identity as an autonomous being. This is hinted at in the opening verse, "Abraham begot Isaac." Impaired of initiative, decisions are being made for him, not by him. A wife is chosen for him, and even dispensing his blessing is engineered by others. Is it any wonder that he had a hidden wish for assertiveness and strength? His preference for Esau is a way of reaching out for a new persona by having an aggressive son, Esau, who represents Isaac's unconscious and unfulfilled wishes for himself. It is a kind of psychological transference, of creating a false façade through favoring a son unlike himself, and thereby becoming the person he wishes to be. When Isaac eats of the venison of his son, Esau, it could be a metaphor for internalizing the wished for aggressiveness and strength of this son. He therefore feels psychologically connected to Esau through this false self-image.

Jacob, on the other hand, has a psychological makeup that is closer to that of Isaac, who like his father is controlled by his mother, Rebeccah, in his growing up years. Perhaps Jacob's attempts to acquire the birthright and Isaac's blessing were motivated not only by religious considerations, but by his need to bolster his self-esteem. Later in life, away from the influence of his mother, Jacob begins to assert himself and demonstrate mature leadership. Jacob's struggle is between the two unspoken messages of his father, one is a conscious demonstration of passivity, and the second is an unconscious wish for assertiveness. Esau picks up Isaac's unconscious wish for aggressiveness whereas Jacob acquires Isaac's quiet compliant disposition. Isaac, never having left home, does not have to face up to his deficits and attain his true potential as does his son Jacob and his father, Abraham. He, therefore, seeks to overcome his passivity vicariously through his son, Esau. It is understandable why Rebeccah favors Jacob, because he is a youthful reminder of the gentle nature that she found attractive in her husband, Isaac. It turns out that not only is Rebeccah the deceptive one, but it is also her husband, Isaac, who in his own quiet way retaliates against his more demonstrative wife, by encouraging Esau to be everything he is not and wishes to be.

It is interesting to note, that unlike his son, Jacob, and his grandson, Joseph, there is no report in the Torah of Isaac having dreams. We know that dreams often contain both wishes and fears. His blindness, therefore, is not just a product of old age, but is in fact a metaphor for his psychological blindness for never allowing himself to see his own unconscious wishes. Consequently, he is not really able to distinguish one child from the other when it comes time for his blessing. What we "see" is not always the concrete image in front of us, but our own preconceived perceptions drawn from our unconscious. And so it is for Isaac. The trauma of the *Akeidah* may have prevented him from finding some outlet for his unconscious desires in the form of dreams. His son, Jacob and grandson, Joseph, however, gain much inspiration from their dreams which is why the Torah records them in such detail as they represent the turning points in their development toward maturity. Isaac, on the other hand, is given short shrift in the Torah's saga of the patriarchs, yet he is an important generational link in tracking the psychological development of the patriarchal family.

Vayeitzei
Genesis 28:10-32:3
Jacob's Dream

*E*n *route to Haran, Jacob lies down in an open field and has a dream of a ladder stretching up to heaven with angels ascending and descending on it. G-d promises this land to him and to the multitude of his future descendants. In gratitude of G-d's protection, Jacob promises Him a tithe of all his possessions. Jacob arrives at a well in Haran where he meets his cousin Rachel. Laban arranges for Jacob to work for him seven years in order to win the hand of his beloved Rachel. At the completion of this period of time, "uncle" Laban substitutes Leah for Rachel with the excuse that she is the older sister. Jacob agrees to work another seven years for the younger Rachel. Leah gives birth to Reuven, Simeon, Levi and Judah in short order, whereas Rachel remains childless. After the concubines, Bilhah and Zilpah, give birth to Dan, Naftali, Gad and Asher respectively, Leah gives birth to Issachar and Zebulun and a daughter Dinah. Rachel finally gives birth to Joseph. In a complicated business arrangement involving their cattle, Laban again attempts to deceive Jacob, but is outwitted by him. Jacob realizes that after twenty years his fortunes have grown to a point that he can no longer coexist with Laban and his envious sons. Jacob decides to leave with his entire family against Laban's wishes. After a tense confrontation, Laban agrees to enter into a covenant of friendship with Jacob who then returns to his ancestral home.*

"Dreams: The Royal Road to the Unconscious"
— Sigmund Freud

The title of this *Parshah*, *Vayeitzei* ("Going Out"), is chosen not only because it is the first word in this week's Torah portion, but because it provides an insight into the whole internal psychological process which Jacob is undergoing. Commentators correctly question, why is it necessary to record from where Jacob is leaving, since it is his destination, Haran, that is most important. *Vayeitzei* is a metaphor for the whole concept of separation, from his early dependent state of development represented by Beersheba, and now going to Haran, representing his development towards becoming a separate adult. This traumatic move is not only a physical one, but a deep emotional one, as Jacob attempts to tear away from parents pulling in different directions and from a brother intent on killing him. Jacob is also struggling with guilt feelings over deposing Esau of the birthright, as well as with his deceptiveness in colluding with his mother in acquiring Isaac's blessing. These conscious forces stalking the lonely guilt-ridden Jacob, fade into his unconscious producing the remarkable dream of a ladder as he lies down to sleep in Beth El.

In the above title, we note one of Freud's great contributions to the science of psychoanalysis, and that is the centrality of dreams in unlocking the unconscious. Even before the appearance of Joseph, acknowledged by Freud as the great interpreter of dreams, we already see in Jacob's ladder dream the remarkable workings of the unconscious. The fact that the dream occurs during his flight from home, lends credence to the notion that Jacob's unconscious is struggling with the complex of family relationships which precipitated his flight. Given that according to Freud, dreams are the royal road to the unconscious, it is well to examine the dream from the perspective of psychoanalysis. One psychoanalytic view of the ladder dream is that of Dorothy Zeligs, who contends that the ladder is a male sexual symbol stretching from mother earth (Rebeccah) to distant G-d in heaven (Isaac), as Jacob's unconscious reacts to the conflict between his mother Rebeccah, and his father Isaac, over his position vis-à-vis Esau in the family structure.

My view, however, is that the dream symbolizes Jacob's internal conflict over the issue of seeking to establish a separate identity and engendering his own ego ideal. The angels going up and down the ladder are symbolic of his internal struggle, framed between the opposing desires of his parents. Only when Jacob can resolve his internal conflict to determine who he really is, can he face his brother Esau, and proceed to hear G-d's message. In Jacob's flight from home, where he was dominated by his mother and ignored by his father, it is reasonable to assume that the internal conflict was a reflection of this identity crisis. What kind of a self-image could Jacob have of himself? On the one hand, he identifies with the negative feminine characteristics of his loving mother Rebeccah, which consist of deception and aggression and on the other, with his father Isaac, marked by passivity and lack of normal aggressiveness.

Fast forward to all Jacob's experiences as a father in Haran, where he succeeds in overcoming his devious uncle Laban, and one can see how he is beginning to mature and to develop a strong sense of self (ego).

This character change is reflected in Jacob's second dream where an angel instructs him about breeding various types of sheep to enable him to attain his appropriate share of the sheep. We see emerging a more mature assertive Jacob who is finally able to leave Laban, "because I [G-d] have seen all that Laban doeth to thee" (Gen. 31:12). This dream is Jacob's unconscious wish to get what he really deserves without having to be devious or deceptive.

Unbeknown to Jacob, this dream also qualifies him to become "the first geneticist." Freud cites a similar type dream of a scientist patient who was deeply troubled because he could not find a solution to a vexing mathematical problem. The patient dreamed of a snake which swallowed its tail. When the patient awoke he recognized this was his unconscious telling him in symbolic language the solution to his mathematical problem. Dreams can demonstrate conflict as in the ladder dream, and can also offer solutions as in Jacob's second dream of sheep. This latter dream is a reflection of Jacob's evolving maturity in that his unconscious is guiding him how to deal forthright with his corrupt Uncle Laban. The two dreams are like bookends, enclosing a period of twenty years of internal psychological development. Now it is time for a more mature Jacob to advance to the next stage, which is reparation of his relationship with his twin brother, Esau. In so doing, he is on his way to discovering who he really is, which was the unconscious wish of the "ladder" dream.

Vayishlach
Genesis 32:4-36:43
The Fear of Esau

*A*s Jacob journeys toward his homeland, he prepares his camp
for the inevitable confrontation with his brother, Esau. That
night, G-d's messenger wrestles with Jacob, and although victorious
he is left impaired. Jacob extracts a blessing from the stranger which
involves a name change from Jacob (supplanter) to Israel (Champion/
Prince of G-d). Jacob and Esau reconcile and go their separate ways.
Jacob encamps in Shechem where he purchases a parcel of land
from Hamor, a local chieftain. Shechem, son of Hamor, is attracted
to Dinah, Jacob's daughter and violates her. Hamor, at the request
of his son Shechem, speaks to Jacob about arranging a marriage
between Shechem and Dinah, as well as joining forces personally
and economically. Dinah's brothers, however, enraged over her
abduction, concoct a plan to have the town males circumcised as
a condition for them to join forces. When most vulnerable, Dinah's
brothers, Simeon and Levi, massacre Shechem and Hamor and
other males in the town. While Jacob was horrified by their actions,
the brothers contend that the dishonor of their sister required this
violent response. Resuming their journey, Rachel dies in childbirth
of a son, Benjamin, the last of the twelve sons of Jacob and is
buried in Bethlehem. Jacob, et al, finally arrive in Hebron home
of his father, Isaac, and grandfather, Abraham. Isaac dies at age
180. The Parshah concludes with a detailed genealogy of the many
descendants of Esau.

Self-Actualization
and Maturity

The Freudian concept characterized as the "adhesiveness of the libido" is aptly dramatized in this *Parshah*. This concept means that we are "glued" to the objects of our past, and driven to repeat certain unresolved issues in our unfinished development. Whatever passes before us in our present life is viewed from the perspective of our past, which prevents us from seeing and dealing with the present. Case in point are the stages of Jacob's inner development as reached in this week's Torah portion. Previously, we read about Jacob's flight from the scene of sibling rivalry with his twin brother, Esau, bereft of physical possessions, but endowed with spiritual assets, the birthright and his father's ill-gotten blessing. During the ensuing twenty years with his uncle Laban, a master of deception, Jacob is again engaged in a variety of scenarios involving Laban's deviousness and deception, e.g., switching of brides and wages. Unable to tolerate this environment any longer, Jacob again resorts to flight, this time to escape from Laban. Now, however, unlike the previous flight, Jacob leaves with a large family laden with cattle and possessions.

There seems to be an unmistakable pattern of behavior repeated by Jacob, deception and flight. What psychological factors can help to explain Jacob's reaching a point in his life when he again needs to escape? It is Freud's insight into human behavior "the adhesiveness of the libido" mentioned above. Despite Jacob's material wealth, the birthright, his mother's love and his father's blessing, Jacob is still struggling with a serious psychological deficit which leaves him feeling empty. We are familiar with the psychological deficit that occurs when someone buys love through gifts, performance or money. Though there may be a short-lived sense of acceptance and success, the person is left with the feeling of being unworthy of being loved just for who he is. The necessity to buy this love leaves the person with the feeling that "more is less" the more one has to do this, the less worthy one feels. The acquisition of the birthright and blessing left Jacob in a more vulnerable psychological state than before, wondering who he really is. Jacob is still stuck with the unfulfilled wish to get the love of his father Isaac. He could not experience the pleasure of lighting up his father's dimmed eyes in the way that he saw Esau was able to do. Moreover, he is still stricken with guilt over deceiving his father with respect to the blessings, albeit orchestrated by his mother Rebeccah. His repeated flight therefore was not only from Esau and Laban, but from his inner self that perpetrated these deceptions. This complex psychological landscape of feelings and conflict sets the stage for that feared moment when Jacob would meet his twin brother after over twenty years of alienation.

The confrontation that follows, pitting Jacob against the man/angel, is truly remarkable in that the Midrash with penetrating psychological insight identifies the angel combatant as, *saro shel Esav*, "the alter ego of Esau." On the eve of meeting his estranged brother, Jacob is still engaged in an internal struggle over the sibling rivalry of his youth. The vanquishing of the angel is really a metaphor for a victory of the unconscious in overcoming his past deceptions and becoming a more honest mature adult. The problem of Jacob's physical lameness resulting from this inner psychological struggle can be explained as a kind of temporary psychosomatic reaction to intense fear. Serious trauma and stress are known to cause these kinds of physical reactions, such as one becoming paralyzed with fear, when unable to flee from an attacker. Here, too, Jacob's inner struggle is that he wants to reconcile with his brother, but is paralyzed with fear and wants to run away. His lameness is his body's response to this deep inner struggle. As a result of this struggle, Jacob finally comes to terms with his past misdeeds, and as his new name "Israel" indicates, he emerges as a transformed individual who has "struggled and overcome." The recognition of his new found resolve and maturity is in Jacob's statement to Esau, "take I pray thee my gift that is brought to thee; because G-d has dealt graciously with me and because I have enough" (Gen. 33:11). Here we see that Jacob no longer feels that he needs more as a substitute compensation for the lost love of his father. Jacob resolves his internal issues of identity, and has come to the realization that he has enough, and is whole. Thus he comes to meet his brother to give, not to take, and being able to say, "I have enough." He no longer needs to manipulate events to gain self esteem from others. Reaching this level of self knowledge is a sign of evolving maturity. Moreover, he feels that G-d has become his substitute father who loves him and who has dealt graciously with him. This Divine blessing is not stolen. He has earned it through hard work, which has restored his view of himself as one who can accomplish by creating his own fortune. Indeed, at this point in his life, he could say, "I have enough," both physically and psychologically. This is a sign of Jacob's giving up the old unresolved yearnings, and is moving in his development toward maturity by being able to deal responsibly with the present.

We conclude this *Parshah*, (before the scene shifts to Joseph), with both brothers recognizing the futility of spending the rest of their lives in competition, each feeling the other has what he is entitled to. Each brother takes his own place as head of a clan in separate areas, knowing they can now function as mature men. The Midrash in its usual insightful manner confirms Jacob's psychological transformation and maturity by commenting on the verse, "And Jacob came in peace [Shalom] to the city of Shechem [after their reconciliation]" (Gen. 33:18). The Hebrew word Shalom is derived from the root *shalem* (whole/unimpaired), meaning that Jacob was a whole new person; physically healed from his lameness, a sign of his overcoming his psychological insecurities, and enjoying peace of mind and body. In Freudian terms, this internal resolution freed up the libido (energy) to be able to use its mature abilities to cope with the present, instead of looking at the present through the distorted lens of the past. This maturation process helped the brothers heal their old wounds. Jacob was able to overcome "the adhesiveness of the libido," for now as Israel, he has matured to a point where he has discovered who he really is. His new identity is a fitting sequel to this quest which was dramatized in the ladder dream in Beth El. As a mature responsible ethical adult and father, he can now direct his libido towards safeguarding the welfare of his large family.

Vayeishev
Genesis 37:1-40:43
Joseph and his Brethren

Now that Jacob has returned home, the Torah focuses on Joseph, his favored son by Rachel, for whom he makes a coat of many colors which incites the animosity of his brothers. To make matters worse, Joseph tells them of his dreams concerning sheaves of corn bowing to his sheaf, and of the sun, moon and stars bowing to him. The brothers plan to kill him, but are dissuaded by Reuven, the oldest of the brothers, who suggests they throw Joseph into a pit. Judah persuades them to extricate Joseph, and sell him to passing merchants. They proceed to dip Joseph's coat into goat's blood in order to deceive their father Jacob into thinking that a wild animal devoured Joseph. Jacob is inconsolable. Joseph is taken to Egypt and sold to Potiphar, Pharaoh's chamberlain. The Torah then shifts its focus to Joseph's brother Judah, who marries a Canaanite woman, who bears him three sons—Er, Onan and Shelah. Judah chooses Tamar as a wife for Er, who dies shortly thereafter. Tamar then marries Onan in levirate tradition, but he too dies without issue. Widowed twice, Tamar is bound to the youngest, Shelah, to await another levirate marriage. In the meantime, Judah's wife, the daughter of Shua dies. Tamar is disheartened that Shelah, although now eligible to marry her, has not done so. Hearing that her father-in-law Judah, is traveling nearby, she disguises herself as a harlot. In the negotiations that follow, Tamar receives several of Judah's personal effects in return for agreeing to have relations with him. Months later, it is reported to Judah that his unwed daughter-in-law Tamar is pregnant. Judah is enraged not realizing that he is the prospective father. When Tamar produces Judah's personal effects, he realizes that he is the father and that he was negligent in his treatment of Tamar. Returning to Joseph, he quickly rises in Potiphar's service to become his household overseer. Potiphar's wife is attracted to Joseph, and when he resists her advances, she falsely accuses him of seducing her. Joseph is jailed and there too, he rises to the top, especially in his ability to interpret the dreams of the jailed wine steward and the baker. Pharaoh's wine steward is released as Joseph predicts, yet forgets to intercede on Joseph's behalf. Joseph remains in jail.

Dreams:
The Power of the Unconscious

As we are introduced to Joseph in this *Parshah* via his dreams of grandeur, one can begin to understand why Freud often referred to himself as Joseph, the interpreter of dreams. His book *Interpretation of Dreams* established his fame as an innovator and synthesizer in the new field of Psychoanalysis. The inspiration for Freud's specializing in this subject could be related to the important role dreams play in the Bible. For example, just as Joseph later in *Parshat Mikeitz* uses numbers as referring to time in interpreting Pharaoh's dreams ("seven good cows are seven years"), so Freud states that numbers in dreams often refer to time in the life of the patient. There are also strong indications that Freud knew of the Talmudic discussions on dreams, since the Tractate *Berachot,* which contains these discussions, was found in his personal library.

Joseph appears on the scene as a lad of seventeen, which in that era would be considered a man. And so, despite his mature perceptions and ability to be in touch with his unconscious via his dreams, we see his immaturity in using these skills to intimidate his brothers, causing intense sibling rivalry. This is evidenced in his dreams of the sheaves and the stars where his grandiosity and narcissism are blatantly demonstrated. Being the second youngest and most favored among the brothers, he is kept infantilized in his father's house where he remains in a state of childlike narcissism. This "all about me" attitude engenders envy and hatred in his brothers.

At this stage, Joseph's situation is analogous to that of a psychologically overburdened child. The elevated position he enjoys, which heightens childhood grandiosity, also places a premature psychological burden upon him. It usually causes anxiety and a false sense of superiority, because he is encouraged to believe what he knows deep inside may not be true. The fantasy of the exaggerated expectations in his dreams is also above his age appropriate abilities. Joseph, at age seventeen, is at a stage when he is neither a child nor an adult.

This all begins to change after Joseph is sold into slavery in Egypt, and especially after his winsome personality leads him to become overseer in the household of Potiphar. Here we begin to see a replay of familiar circumstances whereby Joseph becomes the favored one; this time over his Egyptian counterparts. It culminates when Potiphar's wife attempts to seduce him and make him believe that he is again the special chosen one. His ability to control his aroused sexual feelings earn him, in Judaic sources, the title of *Yosef Ha-Tzaddik* ("Joseph the saint"). From a psychological perspective, however, his actions are not destined for sainthood, but demonstrate a change of character from childhood narcissism to adult maturity. Faced with the danger of a repeat of childish selfish grandiosity, Joseph may have thought of what in popular parlance is known as, "been there done that." This time, Joseph reacts as a responsible moral adult. "There is none greater in this house than I, neither hath he [Potiphar] kept back anything from me but thee, because thou art his wife. How can I do this great wickedness and sin against G-d?" (Gen. 39:9). In his resistance, Joseph demonstrates a remarkable example of being able to control his "id" (impulses) as well as a developed "superego," the Freudian equivalent of conscience. This character transformation will serve him well during his subsequent incarceration for a crime he did not commit. In prison he learns to listen to other people's dreams, e.g., the wine steward and the baker, and more realistically to getting along with other people, while not abandoning his dreams of greatness. He also develops a talent to observe and synthesize what other people say, and what they tell him about their experiences. In this manner, he is able to hone his skill of dream interpretation by "connecting the dots" of the unconscious dream with conscious reality. Joseph is now on the threshold of capitalizing on this developed skill, when destiny will provide the appropriate opportunity.

Mikeitz
Genesis 41:1-44:17
Joseph and Pharaoh

While Joseph is still languishing in jail, Pharaoh has two disturbing dreams about cattle, and about ears of corn. Unable to find anyone who can interpret them, Pharaoh's wine steward remembers Joseph's skill of dream interpretation. Joseph is then released from jail and is summoned before the king. Joseph's interpretation of the dreams as forecasting impending periods of abundance, followed by periods of famine, ring true to the king, who appoints him as overseer of the entire operation of establishing food granaries. As Viceroy of Egypt, Joseph is now given an Egyptian name, and is wed to Asenath, daughter of Poti-phera, priest of On. He is now thirty years of age, and subsequently fathers two sons Manasseh and Ephraim. Meanwhile, Jacob back home in Canaan, is affected by the famine which Joseph had forecast, and decides to send his sons to Egypt to purchase food. Joseph, whose Egyptian name is Tsofnat-Paneah, recognizes his brothers, but they do not recognize him. Remembering his early dreams of superiority over his brothers, Joseph decides to reenact them in real life. He deals harshly with them, accusing them of being spies. He reluctantly releases them, together with all their provisions, while keeping brother Simeon as hostage. This was done to ensure their eventual return with his younger brother, Benjamin. The strategy works, as they are forced to return together with Benjamin because of the continuing severe famine. It is only through the heartfelt intercession of his brother Judah, that Jacob agrees to send his youngest son Benjamin away to Egypt. When Joseph sees his "blood" brother, Benjamin together with the others, he welcomes them warmly into his home as honored guests. He instructs his steward to fill their sacks with all of their provisions, even returning their purchase money as he had done on their previous trip. This time, however, he asks his steward to plant Joseph's silver goblet into Benjamin's sack. No sooner had the brothers left the city together with Simeon, who is newly released, than Joseph orders them to return, on the grounds that someone has stolen his silver goblet. Despite their protestations of innocence, a search ensues and to their horror, the planted goblet is found in Benjamin's sack. Judah, Benjamin's guarantor, is crestfallen, and meekly suggests that they all become slaves to Joseph, recognizing this as G-d's punishment for the whole Joseph fiasco. Joseph demurs, asking only for Benjamin to remain.

The First
Psychoanalytic Referral

Those who are mental health professionals would agree that after one is in practice for a number of years, most of the referrals come by word of mouth from other patients who have undergone successful treatment. This may seem elementary, but what is unusual is that we are privy to exactly this kind of referral in this *Parshah*. Pharaoh is referred to Joseph by a former satisfied "patient," i.e., the wine steward, whose dream Joseph successfully interpreted while together in jail. Here in the Joseph story we now have the first instance of a successful referral. His skill of dream interpretation and personal maturity, are the qualifications which earn his referral to the Pharaoh. The most remarkable and insightful part of his interpretation of Pharaoh's dream about the seven cows is Joseph's statement: "It is not me; G-d will give Pharaoh an answer of peace" (Gen. 41:16).

Here again we see proof of Joseph's maturity in recognizing the limitations of his human powers. Joseph understands by this time that it is not only the content of the dream which is important, but the dreamer himself, how he describes the dream, and what are his associations. We already saw these abilities in the manner in which Joseph interpreted the dreams of the baker and wine steward. Instinctively, Joseph understood what we know today, that a recurring dream within a given time period may involve the same theme, though the symbolism may be different. Accordingly, some of what is current today about dream interpretation was already displayed by Joseph. Freud structured and synthesized methods of dream interpretation, but the ground-breaking creative insights into dream interpretation were already displayed by Joseph. The major difference between them is that unlike Freud, Joseph attributed his powers to a Higher Source.

This *Parshah* gives credence to the prophesy of Joseph's first dreams in *Parshat Vayeishev* about the stars and sheaves of corn. This prophetic dream, however, could not materialize until Joseph is able to go through his own psychological maturation which facilitates the development of the skills of insight inherent in him. Joseph's early dreams are really a reflection of his own psychological state, that of early childhood, when the child experiences himself as the center of the familial universe. During this stage, everyone is attending to him, waiting on him and fulfilling his every desire. During the later maturation stage in Egypt, we find Joseph fulfilling other people's dreams and missions, thinking of others, culminating in the adult stage where he is able to assume the position of responsible leadership for the welfare of all Egyptians.

On this level, Joseph is able to overcome his personal need for retaliation against his brothers, and proceeds to save his family from starvation, notwithstanding the fact that he exposed them to some of the same hardships he suffered at their hands. This stratagem of retaliation is known in Hebrew as *middah ke-neged middah*, colloquially translated as "tit for tat." For example, Joseph was thrown into the pit by his brothers and Joseph retaliates by keeping Simeon hostage. Joseph is favored by his father for which he is rejected by his brothers, Joseph retaliates by favoring his blood brother, Benjamin. The brothers deceive their father about Joseph with the bloody coat and Joseph retaliates by deceiving the brothers with the silver goblet. Nevertheless, these tactics do not stand in the way of granting them complete forgiveness, a further sign of Joseph's mature psychological development.

Vayigash
Genesis 44:18-47:27
Judah's Plea

*J*udah, the brothers' spokesman, makes an impassioned appeal to
Joseph for Benjamin's release to be reunited with his aged, grieving father Jacob, and offering himself in his stead. Joseph is overcome
with emotion, orders the room cleared of all outsiders, and reveals
his true identity as their brother Joseph whom they sold into Egypt.
Joseph explains that the entire scenario was part of G-d's plan to
save the family from starvation. Jacob is dumbfounded when the
brothers return and tell him of Joseph's exalted position in Egypt.
Joseph advises that Jacob and his entire household should now leave
Canaan, and reside in Goshen, Egypt which is conducive for cattle
tending. Jacob agrees to uproot himself and en route to Egypt, G-d
reassures him in a dream, that he is destined to father a great nation
in Egypt. A listing of Jacob's family of seventy souls is recorded. After
twenty-two years of separation, Jacob and Joseph are reunited in a
tearful embrace. Jacob and sons are given an audience with Pharaoh, who recognizes their expertise by appointing them royal offi-
cers, and superintendents of the king's herdsmen. Jacob, in gratitude,
blesses Pharaoh. The Parshah concludes with a description of how
Joseph succeeds in redistributing the land and the people to enable
the country to function during the famine.

The Past, Present and Future: An Unbreakable Bond

It is not unusual to hear people raise the unanswerable conundrum, "why do bad things happen to good people?" Although we do not know the answer to these questions, we do recognize that something that happens in the moment is only a fragment in a total ungraspable picture. Joseph suffers a tragedy. He is sold into bondage for thirteen years, two years of which he spends in prison. Yet what seems like a tragic ending for a promising young man is only the middle piece of the puzzle. The beginning of his future is still not put into its proper place. Joseph must have had many angry depressing thoughts during those years: why did he taunt his brothers; why was he sold as a slave and suffering the feeling of abandonment; and finally, why did his brothers never come to redeem him? It is no wonder that he is so reluctant to make contact with his family for so many years, especially with his father Jacob for whom Joseph showed so much personal concern during the negotiations with his brothers.

Psychoanalysis is a method of intensive treatment not recommended for all patients, especially for those with fragile egos. The reason for this is that it is a deep probing intrusion into the psyche of the individual, whose formation occurs early in the growing up years in one's family. (Not everyone seeking treatment is stable enough to venture into this type of deep psychological introspection.) Parents and siblings exercise a profound influence on a person's subsequent behavior which may cause developmental issues. To appreciate the value of this psychoanalytic approach in the context of Biblical figures such as Jacob and Joseph, (who are not available to lie on the couch and free associate), leaves us with only one option which is to make certain observations based on information provided in the textual narrative. Joseph must have harbored deep feelings of anger toward his father, the dominant figure in the family constellation. By visibly favoring Joseph over his brothers, Jacob not only instigated intense sibling rivalry, but he was repeating the very same parental favoritism to which he was subjected and victimized in his growing-up years. Joseph, who is so psychologically perceptive, must have felt enraged at his father's insensitivity to his plight. Joseph also must have realized that although it was gratifying to be considered "numero uno," he may have questioned his father's motive behind his unusual attachment to him. Was this love for him genuine, or was it somehow a displacement for the missing love Jacob yearned from his father Isaac? The result of the interplay of these complex inter-psychic forces left Joseph with a determination not to renew contact with his father. It is only now, after the maturational impact of his Egyptian experiences, and after his unexpected reunion with his brothers, that Joseph is able to psychologically piece together the facets of his life and become amenable to reconciling with his father.

The idea that one segment of a person's life, extremely positive or negative, can stand by itself is negated both in this week's *Parshah* and in the field of psychology/psychoanalysis. We see that the basis for what happens later in life, or how we deal with issues later in life, has its foundation grounded firmly in the early formative years of our childhood. Freud made the statement that the child who is the "apple of his mother's eye," and who creates a response of great joy in her, will instinctively be prepared to achieve greatness in his own life. We see with Joseph that the parental responses toward him help inspire him to believe that he too is destined for greatness. The recognition that life events may change, and that there will be bumps or trauma along the way, is received by this kind of person as interruptions, but not blockages to the process of fulfilling one's destiny. The happenstance meeting with his brothers is the last piece in the puzzle that confirms Joseph's early dreams. The subsequent traumatic events that he participates in, convince him that they are somehow orchestrated by the hand of G-d. In reaching this stage, Joseph then realizes that the painful piece of his being sold into slavery is another unseen part of G-d's plan. Because of this, he is now able to forgive his brothers and recognize that the present is only a small piece of life's greater puzzle. Without the exploration of the past, however, we cannot really understand our actions and reactions in the present and, therefore, feel we have no control over our futures. When this point is reached in therapy, the patient can stop living in the past as if one is still a victim of unresolved childhood circumstances. Without this psychological exploration, we are like riders in a driverless car, with our unconscious desires driving us to unknown destinations. When Joseph put the pieces together, he could forgive his brothers, and even reward them for helping G-d fulfill his destiny. At the end of this *Parshah*, the circle of the story is completed with the prediction that Joseph will be there to close his father's eyes, bringing completion and closure to each of them. Joseph, who lit up his father's eyes in life, has the *zechut* (merit) to close them in the end.

Vayechi
Genesis 47:28-50:26
Jacob's Final Blessings

The book of Genesis concludes with the death of Jacob at age 147, and the fulfillment of a prior request of Joseph that he be buried in the family sepulcher in Hebron. Prior to his death, Jacob summons his sons to bequeath his blessings upon them, and to foretell, in poetic form, what will befall them in the "end of days." He characterizes the virtues and faults of each of his sons, and what is destined for them when they grow into tribes and settle in the Promised Land. Jacob is disappointed in Reuven, who does not live up to his potential as being firstborn. Likewise, he is disappointed with the volatile tempers of Simeon and Levi, especially their violent behavior in Shechem when avenging the rape of their sister, Dinah. Each of the other brothers receives generally favorable mention by their father. The two who are singled out for lavish praise are Judah and Joseph. Judah's strength of character and sibling leadership are destined to produce a tribe endowed with military and governing authority. Jacob's warmest words are directed to his favored son, Joseph, "the prince of his brethren," who had to overcome the envy and enmity of his brothers. There is here a recognition of Joseph's vision and spiritual strength and his remarkable ability to bring them to fruition. This Parshah and the book of Genesis conclude with the death of Jacob and with the subsequent death of Joseph at age 110. Prior to his death, Joseph reassures his brothers of his good will and willingness to forgive their errant behavior towards him. Joseph is embalmed in Egyptian fashion, and extracts a promise from them to be interred eventually in the Promised Land.

Jacob: The First
Vocational Counselor

As part of religious faith, one is expected to do *teshuvah*, which is often translated as "repentance." This Hebrew term in its root form, *shuv*, really means "return." The question is: return to what? The traditional answer is, return to G-d by fulfilling the precepts of the Torah. One accepts this duty as a partner with G-d, based on the *brit*, mutual covenant with the Almighty entered into by the patriarch, Abraham. In order to become a true partner, one must, however, first look into oneself, i.e., introspection, a process which is highlighted during the High Holidays. This process of introspection entails an internal psychological quest which, as we have seen, Jacob/Israel has successfully accomplished.

In this week's *Parshah* we see a demonstration of this process of introspection, as Jacob addresses his sons on his death bed. He displays the ability to evaluate his relationship with his sons, and to see the distinct character traits of each one of them as separate individuals. This is a transformed Jacob/Israel, who no longer views his son Joseph as his narcissistic love object engendering the enmity of his other sons. Through Jacob's internal search and life experiences, he can "return" to his position as an objective father who is able to perceive his sons as they really are, and not as objects for his own narcissistic needs. For example, in the blessing of his firstborn, Reuven, Jacob is able to see both sides of his character. He acknowledges Reuven's first born status, yet recognizes his limitations "unstable as water" (Gen. 49:4), and, therefore, Reuven must forfeit his position as family leader. Similarly with

Simeon and Levi, Jacob deplores their kinship of violence, thereby disqualifying them from future leadership, albeit Levi did later become the progenitor of the priestly clan. The characteristics that Jacob sees in his first three sons of instability, rage and violence, are not unusual in children who are overburdened by their father. This is the price Jacob has to pay because of his own character flaws which obviously affected these three sons. Upon these three oldest brothers, the parental impact was apparently strongest, for we see that the rest of the brothers were less negatively affected and thereby merited the approbation of their father.

Of special interest is Jacob's most positive blessings given to Judah and Joseph. Joseph is able, through his internal struggles and insight, to remove the distraction of the multi-colored coat, i.e., his narcissistic display for attention, and convert it into healthy leadership with an ability to concern himself with the welfare and needs of others. In so doing, he is able to solidify his authentic identity and retain the internalized family goals and values despite the allure of Egyptian society. His acknowledgment, "I was stolen from the land of the Hebrews" (Gen. 40:15), reflects Joseph's unconscious yearning to return to his roots. The return to his authentic self is the necessary condition for becoming whole, whereby Joseph now recognizes that he is a partner with G-d in carrying out His plan.

Judah, who emerges as the spokesman and leader of his brothers, demonstrates an acute awareness of self, when he declares, "she [Tamar] is more righteous than I" (Gen. 38:26). He displays maturity in saying, "Your servant is responsible for the lad" (Gen. 44:32), and concern for others by saying: "take me as a slave but let the lad [Benjamin] return with his brothers" (Gen. 44:33). He is also a decision maker who recognizes the importance of law/structure, "I gave her [Tamar] not to my son Shelah" thus anticipating the law of levirate marriage. Jacob recognizes these leadership characteristics in his son, Judah, when he declares "the scepter shall not depart from Judah and the legislator's staff from between his legs" (Gen. 49:10).

Joseph and Judah become prime examples of individuals, who like their father, Jacob, struggle internally in order to solidify their identities, enabling them to become the leaders of their brothers. In so doing, they overcome their narcissistic desires, thereby helping to shape the destiny of their descendants. Jacob, in this closing chapter of his life, has come "full circle" in his own personal odyssey, endowed with the insight to objectively evaluate his sons' character traits and forecast their future destinies as they unfold in the succeeding books of the Torah.

THE BOOK OF EXODUS

"Now these are the names of the sons of Israel,
who came into Egypt with Jacob"
— *Exodus* 1:1

Shemot
Exodus 1:1-6:1
Israel Enslaved in Egypt

*A*fter Joseph's death, the descendants of the patriarch Jacob proliferate in Egypt at an alarming rate. Pharaoh, fearing their increasing numbers, enslaves them and orders Hebrew midwives to kill all newborn Hebrew males. In order to save her newborn son, Moses, Yocheved puts him in a basket on the Nile River under the watchful eye of his older sister, Miriam. Pharaoh's daughter, seeing the basket, takes pity on Moses although realizing that he is a Hebrew. Miriam suggests to her that Moses' mother, Yocheved, become his nursemaid and help raise him. Years later, Moses, now an Egyptian prince, sees a taskmaster beating a Hebrew slave, and proceeds to kill him. To escape the wrath of Pharaoh, he flees to Midian where he is taken in by Jethro, the priest, and marries his daughter Zipporah. One day, in shepherding sheep at Mt. Sinai, he witnesses a bush on fire without being consumed. He hears G-d's voice urging him to become the liberator of the Hebrews, a responsibility he reluctantly accepts. After a life-threatening experience involving the circumcision of his newborn son, Moses is reunited with his brother Aaron. Together they confront Pharaoh, with the more articulate Aaron serving as spokesman. They demand that the Hebrews be freed, and be allowed to worship the G-d of Israel. Pharaoh rejects their pleas, and retaliates by imposing even harsher restrictions on the Hebrew slaves. As Moses predicted, the people are greatly disillusioned with his mission. He is, however, encouraged by G-d's reassurance that Pharaoh will be forced to free the Hebrew slaves.

A "Basket Case"
Becomes G-d's Chosen One

In the book of *Bereshith* (Genesis), we see how G-d's covenant with Abraham is transmitted by the patriarchs from father to son. This paternal role model becomes internalized into Israel's belief system of having a powerful G-d father figure who could lead, change and control fate. In the first chapter in *Shemot* (Exodus), we are reminded of this strong father-son bond, when it states, "These are the names of the sons of Israel who came into Egypt with Jacob" (Exod. 1:1), but the names of their female spouses are not mentioned. However, when Jacob's offspring multiplied in Egypt into their respective tribes, we begin to see a subtle shift from this male dominated world, with the appearance of Moses in the basket of bulrushes floating on the Nile River. He is immediately surrounded by female figures. He is rescued by the Egyptian princess through the intervention of Moses' sister Miriam, and is nursed by his mother, Yocheved. He is adopted as a son by the Egyptian princess, and grows up as an Egyptian prince in this female dominated environment. Like many adopted children, Moses goes out of his way to identify with his biological roots by mingling in the fields with his Israelite slave brethren. The intense rage Moses displays when seeing the mistreatment of his kinsmen, results in his slaying of the Egyptian taskmaster. This extreme reaction could be a displacement for his own sense of unfair treatment in being, to some extent, abandoned by his parents. Unlike his older siblings Miriam and Aaron, he was taken away as an infant and raised in alien surroundings albeit in royal luxury. There is no mention in the text of any attempt by older brother Aaron or his father Amram to provide guidance during these crucial formative years.

His differing view of Egyptian and Hebrew males must have contributed to Moses' problem of relating to Hebrew male figures. Hebrew males were seen to be weak, compliant, passive and bereft of leadership. Egyptian males were seen to be privileged, powerful and cruel, as represented by their taskmasters. This mental set would help explain Moses' initial reluctance of trust in a strong male G-d figure who would later reach out to him at Mt. Horeb. It is only in his flight to Midian where Moses first meets Jethro, the Midianite priest who would become his father-in-law, that Moses meets a strong father figure who would give him guidance, empathy and structure. This is borne out when they are later reunited, and Moses greets him warmly, and accepts Jethro's sage advice, "And Moses listened to the voice of his father-in-law and did all that he had said" (Exod. 18:24). This strong father figure, in contrast to his upbringing by female figures, helps convince Moses to accept G-d's call at the burning bush for him to lead the Israelites out of Egypt.

The symbolism of the burning bush is subject to many Midrashic interpretations, but from a psychological perspective, one may view this scene in relation to Moses' emotional state at that period in his life. Moses is "consumed" with an ongoing "burning" anger. Here he is an Egyptian prince, suffering the humiliation of being a displaced refugee, in addition to his anger at being alienated from his family of origin. Moreover, he is beset with internal issues of dual identity, of being both an Egyptian prince and an Israelite. At this point in his life, Moses' self-esteem is at its lowest ebb, as we see in his self-effacing response to the Divine call, "Who am I that I should go to Pharaoh?" (Exod. 3:11) This response, "Who am I," is typical of adopted children. In my practice, I was treating a patient who was adopted by parents who had other natural children. He was constantly angry and troubled because he could "never be real" like the other biological children of his parents. Moses' reply, "Who am I," is not just a sign of undue modesty, but an anguished cry and quest into his true identity. The enigmatic burning bush, when painted on this canvas of turmoil in Moses' soul, is therefore symbolic of his ongoing "consuming" struggles with all of these "fiery" emotional issues.

Who am I?

No sooner did Moses return to his family in Midian after experiencing this life transforming revelation at Mt. Horeb/ Sinai, than we see the immediate psychological impact and repercussions of his new mission. We read about what seems to be an unrelated episode that Bible commentators are hard put to explain. After gathering his family together to embark on his life changing mission, Moses incurs the wrath of the Lord, "The Lord confronted him and wanted to kill him" (Exod. 4:24). What accounts for G-d's violent reaction against his recently chosen liberator? Why is Moses derelict in carrying out the important religious covenant of circumcision upon his newborn son? When viewed from a physical/psychological perspective, however, one can begin to understand Moses' reluctance to shed blood. It would be a reminder of the reason why he is a refugee; his inability to control his rage, and the resulting killing of the Egyptian taskmaster. His wife seeing his paralyzed state, takes matters into her own hands as stated, "Then Zipporah took a flint and cut off the foreskin of her son, and cast it at his [Moses'] feet; and she said: "You are my *hatan damim* [my bridegroom of blood]" (Exod. 4:25). This is a rebuke to her husband, implying that he fled to Midian with blood on his hands, and now, when it comes to shedding the blood of his son in commitment to the service of G-d, he is completely immobilized. It is to this character imperfection that God is reacting in nearly aborting Moses' mission.

It is not unusual for people to cope with forbidden feelings and anxiety, by using intra-psychic methods of denying, distancing and acting in ways that are diametrically opposed to these dangerous impulses. Moses, facing his memory of unbridled murderous rage against the Egyptian taskmaster, uses this reaction formation to disconnect from these uncomfortable feelings of aggression and guilt. He sees himself now as a passive man devoid of ambition. When G-d asks him to lead, Moses asks, "Who am I." When his wife asks him to circumcise his son, he becomes paralyzed. This form of unconscious self-deceit allows him to view himself with more favor, by hiding the aggression and murderous rage within himself. To a certain extent we might say Moses undergoes an instant course of anger management with G-d as it were, acting as his therapist. His aggression though never extinguished, is tamed and later sublimated into firm leadership ability. The symbol of anger is fire which is generally interpreted as a powerful force. The burning bush becomes the turning point in Moses' character development, by converting his passion, a positive force, into strong leadership that is not consumed. The issue of harnessing and sublimating aggressive forces into assertive and constructive abilities is the growth process Moses is undergoing in this episode. The fact that this violent episode of circumcision occurs in the lodging place "on the road from Midian to Egypt," supports this psychological interpretation. "On the road" suggests that this marks the character transition of Moses, from the sedentary life of a shepherd in Midian, to that of a new personality burdened with the monumental responsibility of leadership of his kinsmen in Egypt. Yet, in the concise style of Biblical narrative, (this entire circumcision episode consists of only three verses), this overpowering emotional episode is followed immediately with Moses' reuniting with his estranged brother, Aaron, as if nothing momentous had happened. The reader is given only a glimpse of the tremendous inner struggle Moses must have endured in sublimating his untamed passions into energizing his new mission.

He would need to spend the rest of his life learning how to cope with his tempestuous nature, and in so doing, becoming the greatest of all the prophets of Israel. Moses, therefore, becomes the quintessential prototype of character change, symbolized by the "burning bush," for a people who would likewise need to undergo a similar process of transformation, from a "stiff-necked" slave people to a free and independent nation.

Va'eira
Exodus 6:2-9:35
Promise of Redemption

*I*n order to impress Pharaoh with G-d's power, Moses and Aaron
perform various feats, culminating in inflicting upon the Egyptians
what were to become the ten plagues. The first plagues of blood and
frogs are matched by the Egyptian magicians, so that Pharaoh is
unmoved, or as described in this portion of the weekly Torah reading,
"his heart was hardened." Even when the magicians acknowledged
that subsequent plagues could only have been inflicted by the G-d of
Israel, Pharaoh continues to reject Moses' petition for freedom. The
Hebrews living in Goshen are miraculously spared from the effects
of these plagues. As the severity of the plagues increase, Pharaoh
reluctantly begins to grant partial concessions, but Moses insists that
the complete release of the Hebrews is unconditional.

What's in a Name?

In this *Parshah*, G-d gives us a psychological insight into the naming process. In the previous *Parshah*, G-d in answering Moses' question as to His name, describes Himself, "I am Who/ That I am." This "name" illustrates in its vagueness, that G-d is unique in not being nameable. In other words, G-d is saying, "I am Who I [really] am" (Exod. 3:14), unlike humans who struggle their whole lives trying to discover their true identities. It is important for man to evolve and create an identity that is internally anchored, authentic and distinct. G-d, on the other hand, knows who He is. He can, therefore, assume different roles without fear of losing His identity. Accordingly, the Talmud records G-d having seventy different names depending on the roles He plays in varying circumstances, e.g., Father, King, Creator, Lord of Hosts, etc. G-d is saying to mankind, look into yourselves, know who you really are, hold firm to that identity, while being flexible enough to deal with others in a mature way without sacrificing your principles and ideals.

Another way of examining G-d's identity in the expression "I am Who I am" is from a linguistic standpoint. W.W. Meissner, a psychoanalyst, writes about the importance of a child's linguistic awareness in promoting psychological growth, especially in separating from the mother. The child's ability to use the first person, "I," is the first step in establishing a sense of self and separate autonomy. This in turn, leads to the child's ability to engage in dialogue with the second person, "you." In dealing with the enslaved Israelites who are psychologically on an infantile level, it is sufficient for G-d to introduce Himself as "I" who is separate and distinct from "you," (a variant of the "I-Thou" relationship

83

of Martin Buber). Who I am, therefore, is not determined by any confining name, but My identity will evolve through your (Moses') mission and My (G-d's) subsequent actions.

In therapy, one of the major tasks of the therapist is getting the patient to recognize one's authenticity, instead of trying to be like someone else. For example, in the growing family the child complies in order to win the approval of parents. If the parent, however, needs the child to be something for the parent, a "flower in the parent's lapel," the child outwardly assumes the mantel the parent wants, but hides and does not develop his authentic self. This child grows up feeling like an empty shell, often seething with anger and shame that he does not understand. He becomes like a chameleon with the disease to please, yet never feels internally fulfilled.

Another type of externalized identity is that which is developed by the child in response to adolescent peer pressure. We often hear the adolescent taunt parents with the familiar refrain, "everybody else is doing it (drinking, smoking, etc.), so why can't I?" The parent, who can resist this form of peer pressure, is helping the child to individualize, and to develop his own unique personality in order to counteract negative forces in the environment. When the adolescent reaches adulthood, in times of stress, he will again be faced with an identity crisis. Prior parental guidance, or lack of it, will determine whether he has developed the kind of ego to make mature decisions, or remain arrested at an immature stage. This growing up situation is analogous to the psychological state we now find the Israelites in their stage of development. They need to define their identity as a separate G-d chosen people, instead of being a mass of dependent slaves or objects driven by external authority figures.

This understanding of the need for establishing their true identity is being played out in this *Parshah* in the scenario of the ten plagues, with Moses and Pharaoh acting as the key protagonists. We have already seen in Genesis, the Divine plan of keeping Israel physically separate from the Egyptians by locating them in Goshen. This was designed to preserve their separate identity as Jacob's descendants, and prevent them from becoming physically overwhelmed by the dominant forces of the Egyptian culture. This situation prevailed until we are told, "There arose a new king [Pharaoh] who knew not Joseph" (Exod. 1:8). They were then forced to abandon their Israelite identities by becoming Egyptian slaves. (This is not unlike the mentality fostered by the Nazis in dehumanizing their victims.) After 210 years of enslavement, the Israelites are in danger of losing their G-d-chosen covenanted identity, into believing that all power is now vested in humans, and that Pharaoh is the supreme god. It will, therefore, take great acts such as the ten plagues, which are less intended to punish the Egyptians than to convince the Israelites of their true identity by reminding them of their G-d's superior power.

This understanding of the need to reinforce Israel's true identity underlies the repeated statement that "G-d hardened Pharaoh's heart." Why was this necessary? G-d could have just as easily softened his heart to submit and free the slaves. G-d hardened Pharaoh's heart so it would provide repeated opportunities to demonstrate to the Israelites that, "I am Who I am"—a Power over all other powers. This lesson is not only intended for Pharaoh, but more so for the helpless, downtrodden, assimilated Israelites who had forgotten who they really were. This is particularly evident in the fourth plague of "wild beasts or beetles," where it states, "And I shall set apart in that day the land of Goshen, in which my people dwell, that this plague shall not be there, to the end that thou mayest know that I am the Lord in the midst of the earth"(Exod. 8:18). This statement is clearly intended to impress the Israelites of G-d's identity as their saving power.

It is now up to the Children of Israel to live up to its name, which means to "struggle and overcome" as did Jacob in winning this appellation when wrestling with G-d's messenger. (See *Parshat Vayishlach*). A name implies boundaries, as it defines and distinguishes one person from another and one nation from another. Israel is now reaching a stage in its development when it is necessary to follow in G-d's example of uniqueness. They, like their namesake patriarch, Jacob/Israel, will have to struggle mightily in order to shed their dependent slave identity into winning G-d's designation of them as the Chosen People.

Bo

Exodus 10:1-13:16

The Last Plagues

*A*fter various vicissitudes in the negotiations between Moses and Pharaoh, the land of Egypt is decimated by the latter plagues of locusts and darkness. In desperation, Pharaoh issues an ultimatum to Moses and Aaron never to return to the palace upon pain of death. Moses departs with a warning to Pharaoh of the impending last plague, the demise of all first born Egyptian males of humans and animals. The object of all of the plagues as repeated in these weekly readings is to impress upon Pharaoh his acknowledgment of the supremacy of the G-d of Israel.

At this point, the narrative is interrupted with instructions relating to the impending exodus. The month of Nisan, marking the period of the exodus, is declared to be the first of the months in the new lunar calendar. Laws regarding the offering of the paschal lamb are instituted in commemoration of G-d's passing over (Passover) their homes during the scourge of the Egyptian firstborn. Connected with these rituals, are the laws against having any form of leavening hametz during the Passover festival, in commemoration of their hasty departure from Egypt. In this portion, is the law governing the redemption of the first born Jewish male—pidyon ha-ben—in commemoration of the miracle of their safety during the plague of the first born Egyptian males. Also reminiscent of the exodus is the law of Tefillin (phylacteries), which contain references to the exodus. The Parshah concludes with Pharaoh's call to Moses and Aaron, "Rise up, go forth from among my people, both you and the children of Israel and go serve the Lord as you have said" (Exod. 12:31).

Who is Master
and Who is Slave?

One of the perplexing questions regarding this Parshah, is why Pharaoh is punished with the ten plagues, since it is G-d who "hardened" his heart thereby preventing him from freeing the slaves? While in Biblical language Pharaoh's resistance is referred to as "hardening of the heart" in psychological terminology a similar statement is "my emotions have turned to stone." By this the patient usually means, "I do not feel anything, nor can I respond to the affect of others". This condition is often the result of severe trauma or emotional hurt, when the person is afraid to re-experience one's own feelings or display empathy for others. The patient has built a "brick wall" as a defense to protect oneself from re-experiencing the trauma. The rigidity of the wall tells us something about the intense feelings being pushed away. Many of the patient's responses are characterized by the word "no", which is an automatic protective device. Imagine the emotional trauma that Pharaoh (who viewed himself as a god) must have felt, to be in a position to plead with his slave subject Moses to intervene with G-d to remove the plagues! We can now better understand what the text means when it says, "G-d hardened Pharaoh's heart." It is a defense mechanism to prevent him from feeling any compassion for the Israelites whom he regarded as mere objects for exploitation. Pharaoh has lost his power, so his defenses are up, or in Biblical terms, his heart is hardened i.e. he is unable to cope with his inner feelings. He is no longer master over himself, but a slave to his own defenses, as he has lost his free will and is a subject to the G-d of the Israelites.

Contrast this condition with the Israelites, who witnessing the ten plagues afflicting the Egyptians, begin to recognize G-d's superior power, and with it the hope for empowerment and freedom to strive for nationhood. The challenges they had to face were nevertheless difficult ones, leaving their physical home to which they had become accustomed for over 200 years, and to reorient their psyches from a state of psychological dependence and helplessness to one of independence and freedom of will. This sadomasochistic relationship between master and slave, between captor and victim would need much time and work to overcome. The plagues are strong medicine designed to insure the onset of this psychological process. They are now faced with the opportunity to choose a new life as a nation with a new calendar, where time would be under their control. With opportunity comes responsibility, a key factor in moving toward maturity. They are now embarking on the first step in this direction. It is ironic, however, that at this point in their history the Israelites are the ones with the freedom of choice, whereas Pharaoh is the one who is enslaved.

The rest of the *Parshah* begins to flesh out an initial program of individual responsibilities designed to fill the vacuum created between the polarities of Egyptian slavery (dependence) and their new found freedom (independence). The first item on the agenda is preparing the paschal lamb. The sacred lamb of Egypt is now to be sacrificed to the G-d of Israel in preparation for the exodus. The Israelites are, however, not yet ready for self responsibility after so many years of slavery. Moses' strong leadership added to G-d's display of power in executing the ten plagues , is the first step in getting the Israelites to switch allegiances from Egypt to the G-d of Israel. The sacrifice of the paschal lamb, the killing of one of the sacred gods of Egypt, allows each Israelite to feel a sense of participation in the destruction of Egyptian power over them. G-d, seeing their participation by smearing the blood of the paschal lamb on their door-posts, passes over the Israelites during the tenth plague—killing of the Egyptian first born. They have now assumed the first step in accepting responsibility for their own behavior as a free people.

It is neither a random act or coincidence that the sacrificing of the paschal lamb coincides with the killing of the Egyptian first born. The sacrifice of the paschal lamb enacts the killing of one of the gods of Egypt. G-d's killing of the firstborn Egyptians is also directed at the elimination of future generations of Egyptian god-kings. This concurrent act demonstrates that this oppressed people could regain a sense of power by destroying old images. The image of G-d's power in killing the firstborn, matched by sacrificing the paschal lamb, is a concrete display of their own personal power to overcome their sense of helplessness. They are now ready to make the physical break from Egyptian slavery toward freedom, but the psychological break from Egypt by this generation of the exodus would prove to be far more difficult.

Beshallach

Exodus 13:17-17:16

Liberation from Egypt

*T*he Israelites begin their journey to the Promised Land by taking the longer wilderness route in order to avoid confronting the powerful Philistines who are entrenched on the shorter Mediterranean route. They are enjoying G-d's protection and guidance by day with a cloud, and with a pillar of fire at night. In the meantime, Pharaoh begins to regret their emancipation, and marshals his forces to retrieve the Hebrew slaves. The confrontation occurs at the Reed Sea which is miraculously parted to permit the crossing of the Israelites, while the Egyptian forces drown in the returning waters. Inspired by their dramatic escape, Moses and the children of Israel compose a beautiful song. The Sabbath when this song is read in the synagogue is known as Shabbat Shirah (Sabbath of Song). As they proceed on their journey, the Israelites are quickly introduced to the harsh realities of the wilderness, especially in the absence of food and water. They complain bitterly to Moses for leading them out of Egypt. G-d responds by supplying them with heavenly Manna. Moses sweetens the brackish waters at Marah and extracts water from a rock at Meribah. The Parshah concludes with Moses, aided by Joshua, successfully fending off the troublesome attacking Amalekites, who warrant the eternal enmity of the children of Israel.

Separation and Individuation: A Model for Human Development

That which we saw in Moses' character development, stemming from severing his Egyptian roots, is now unfolding with the people as well. It is now necessary for the Israelites to sever their familiar Egyptian roots of 210 years in order to carry out the greater mission and destiny which Moses has set before them, entering the Promised Land. There is, however, one major stumbling block in the path of these recently emancipated slaves. There is no guiding structure, as the Torah has not as yet been given to them. The setting of boundaries to protect the infrastructure of freedom has not as yet been put into place. Their immediate goal at this point is merely physical survival in a foreboding wilderness. Their situation is analogous to families who provide the basic physical necessities of life, but do not provide the structure and discipline needed in raising secure children. These children who are yet unable to verbalize their internal deficits, very often become subject to filling their emptiness with external excesses in food, drink, etc. They get acted out in the form of "give me something to prove you love me." In a sense, this describes the psychological state of the Israelites at this stage of their development. Regression to the "fleshpots of Egypt" now becomes a recurrent theme in the absence of food and water. The security of home life, such as it was in Egypt, is being disrupted as they are forced suddenly to wander aimlessly in the wilderness. The nomadic life which characterized the patriarchs is being reenacted centuries later by their descendants.

From a psychological perspective, however, this stage the Israelites find themselves in as an "infantile" nation may be considered a blessing in disguise. Separation from their Egyptian roots, as painful as it is, affords them the psychological opportunity for individuation as a new people under G-d's protection with Moses serving as the nurturing parent. In fact, this process actually began in the era of the patriarchs and matriarchs. Beginning with Abraham, it was necessary for him to leave his family in Haran, and shed his former identity of "Abram" in order to establish his new greater identity of "Abraham" bestowed upon him by Divine blessing. His son Isaac, on the other hand, the more sedentary of the patriarchs, who never left Canaan, could never realize his potential as a family leader. His son Jacob, however, renewed the Divine call made to his grandfather Abraham, by leaving his parents home in order to establish his new and greater identity as the patriarch "Israel". Through his twelve sons/tribes of Israel; what began as a growing family, through the process of separation and individuation, now becomes a separate and distinct people. However, their 210 year "sojourn" in Egypt threatens to undermine their separate identity. The prosaic statement, "you can take the person out of the country, but not the country out of the person," has psychological wisdom borne out by the Israelite experiences in Egypt. Assimilation into the culturally advanced Egyptian civilization begins to erode their patriarchal memory. Their reluctant entry into the vast wilderness is symbolic of the vast psychological distance they would need to travel in order to divest themselves of their slave mentality and regain their individuality as a separate nation. Only then can they be able to enter the Promised Land, representing a new stage in their developing maturity and independence.

The first stage of developmental separation within the family structure usually occurs between two and four years of age. In this stage, the child tries to form a meager sense of a separate self by saying "no" or "I will do it myself." It is often difficult for parents of these young children to cope with their many tantrums, but they are important events in the establishment of psychological identity. You can observe this in this *Parshah*, in this earliest stage of separation from Egypt. The Israelites rebel against their surrogate "mother" Moses, in favor of their motherland, Egypt. Another key stage of separation and individuation occurs later, during adolescence. The adolescent often tries to form a new identity separate from the parents, which becomes more consolidated during the late adolescent and college years. After graduation from college, it is not unusual for young people to enter a stage when they suddenly discover and acknowledge that their parents have experience and wisdom. At this point, their maturity enables them to adapt their life style more in line with that of their parents, especially when they marry and become parents themselves.

In this *Parshah* we see a similar emergence of difficult issues associated with this maturation process, in the development of the Israelites into a separate new nation. The Torah describes a wandering childlike people, focusing on their physical needs of food and water, looking constantly to their surrogate parent, Moses, for immediate gratification. They are as yet not mature enough to express thanks and appreciation to G-d for their new-found freedom. They constantly regress to their infantile roots, with the familiar refrain "let us go back to Egypt." Even it they were miserable there, they had the security of being told what to do and how to do it. What is most threatening to them at this stage is the fear of change, and assuming individual responsibility in confronting the new circumstances and challenges of freedom. Most of the ensuing issues are tied to this struggle as individuals and as a nation to overcome this fear of change and assuming responsibility for their actions. Accordingly, the sequence of events that follow: splitting of the Reed Sea, sweetening the waters at Marah, being provided with Manna and quail, overcoming the Amalekites all have physical and psychological ramifications. After weathering each crisis, the Israelites regress to their familiar "griping" behavior, instead of acknowledging the supernatural means by which they are saved. The reason for this repetitive behavior is that the source of their problems is not only physical, famine and thirst, but fear of change and parental abandonment, i.e., Moses/G-d. Moses himself, a victim of early family separation is hard put to cope with the anger and complaints of his extended family, the Israelites. Whereas succeeding trying events reveal Moses' ability to overcome his psychological deficits, the Israelites are experiencing great difficulty and psychological resistance to the challenges of freedom.

Jethro
Exodus 18:1-20:23
The Ten Commandments

Their journey continues as they reach the Sinai desert, site of where G-d revealed Himself to Moses at the burning bush. He welcomes his visiting father- in-law, Jethro, and is reunited with his wife, Zipporah, and his two sons, Gershom and Eliezer. Jethro, seeing how much Moses is over-burdened, serving as both leader and supreme judge of such a contentious people, advises him to adopt a hierarchical judicial system assisted by a network of lower judges. Moses accepts the advice and afterwards bids farewell to Jethro. They arrive at the foot of Mt. Sinai, where instructions are given to prepare the people for the dramatic revelation to follow. Moses ascends the mountain amidst thunder and lightning which accompany the giving of the Ten Commandments. The people are in such a state of shock and awe at the experience of Divine revelation that they ask Moses to serve as intermediary. The Parshah concludes with instructions on erecting an altar for future worship of G-d.

The Ten Commandments:

Building Internal as well as External Boundaries

The giving of the Ten Commandments, which is the highlight of this week's Torah reading "Jethro" (and for some, of the entire Torah), is according to some Bible commentators out of proper sequence. They claim that Jethro's suggested judicial system described in this week's *Parshah*, must have occurred after the revelation at Sinai, when the people would then need judges to guide them in the interpretation of the new law (Ten Commandments), rather than before the revelation as it appears in our text. However, from a psychological perspective, Jethro's suggested judicial infrastructure did occur prior to the revelation. The reason being that in human development there needs to be an external structure already in place in order to guide individual behavior. For example, in the family structure, the parents are the authority figures who set boundaries, institute a value system, and provide a sense of discipline and control that the child cannot provide for himself. In the ensuing developmental stages, the child takes over more and more responsibilities, as he internalizes the value system and external boundaries set by the parents and makes them his own. Similarly, here in Jethro's judicial system, we have in place the infrastructure needed in order to implement the forthcoming moral law. This is especially necessary for a mass of recently freed slaves who are as yet incapable of serving as mature adult role models for their children. Jethro fills this vacuum by enlisting the more mature leaders to serve as judges to adjudicate all kinds of relationship issues, relieving Moses of this onerous task.

We also see here the astute psychological insights of Jethro. He advocates a judicial infrastructure built as a pyramid from the simple to the complex. "And let them [judges] judge the people at all times; and it shall be, that every great matter they shall bring to you [Moses], but every small matter they shall judge themselves" (Exod. 18:22). In this manner, Jethro is teaching the people the mechanics of how boundaries work, a kind of training ground for growth in relating to others. This concept is reminiscent of Robert Frost's famous observation that "good fences make good neighbors." What Jethro proposes, through his judicial infrastructure, is the means whereby Moses and the seventy elders (precursor of the *Sanhedrin*) can properly interpret and implement the seeds of G-d's law represented by the Ten Commandments. G-d is presenting a design of boundaries that would not only regulate the external relationship between man and G-d and man to man, but the very inner psychological impulses of the individual by stating what is permissible and what is not. Just as in the physical creation of the world, G-d established the principle of order, similarly, in creating the moral law, the Ten Commandments addresses the need for order in the developmental growth of human kind.

The Ten Commandments addresses this basic need to regulate human behavior by introducing the principle of boundaries, both external and internal. The first five commandments deal largely with external boundaries relating to man's behavior in relation to G-d, e.g., ban on idolatry, prohibiting using His name in vain, and observing His Sabbath. Honoring of parents, the fifth commandment, completes the first set, since parents are G-d's representatives in setting the boundaries for their children. The second set of five, prohibitions on murder, adultery, stealing, misrepresenting and lusting, relate to one's inner struggle with controlling impulses of greed, lust, and aggression. The purpose of the Ten Commandments is to teach human beings to control and overcome their internal instincts which, when left un-checked, would destroy their relationship to G-d and peaceful coexistence with their fellow man.

The key element in this Decalogue, from the standpoint of developmental growth, is contained in the fifth commandment:, "Honor thy father and mother that thy days may be long upon the land which the Lord thy G-d giveth thee" (Exod. 20:12). The wording of this commandment has important psychological implications. It states to honor (*kabed*), not love your parents, which demonstrates, again, the Torah's psychological insight into human behavior. You cannot mandate the emotion of love, but one can structure honorable and respectful behavior toward one's parents. It is also noteworthy that this is the only one of the ten commandments that includes a reward for its observance, namely, "length of days" (longevity). Why is this so? Here we have another example of a question which can benefit from a psychological understanding of filial relationships. If a child is unable to detach his libido from his parents during the appropriate developmental stages, he remains an underdeveloped adult. The pressure to be constantly focused on one's parents creates internal tension preventing further developmental growth. This type of parental attachment is not love, but a burdensome duty causing one to remain stuck in an infantilized psychological "rut." The body translates this tension into stress upon the person's immune system which can lead to physical symptoms such as high blood pressure and other stress related illnesses. Resolving this love/ hate relationship in a way that allows one to relate to one's parents "respectfully," by leading a separate life yet connected in age appropriate ways, is what the wording of the fifth commandment seems to imply. The ability to manage the filial relationship, without the internal stress, frees the libido to lead a longer more psychologically healthy life style. The length of days is, therefore, not only quantitative, but qualitative as well.

The efficacy of the above statement was highlighted to me when supervising a clinical psychologist who specialized in treating Indian couples. The traditional family structure in India is matriarchal. The young married couple usually moves in with the husband's mother, who then becomes the bride's arch competitor for the husband's affection and attention. The mother and her son become the major figures in this triangular relationship, leaving the wife basically abandoned emotionally. The dependent infantilized husband, who is so special to the mother, cannot express anger to this controlling mother, so he displaces it upon his wife. This over attachment to the mother causes tension, shame and rage, which get acted out in inappropriate ways such as infidelity. While this is an example of an Indian cultural phenomenon, it has echoes in other ethnic groups as well. It, however, demonstrates the wisdom of the fifth commandment which focuses on a more mature behavioral relationship of respect rather than on the emotional aspect of love, which can lead to serious marital complications.

It is in this familial arena of the fifth commandment that we have already seen displayed so much of the interplay of these behavioral and emotional forces, especially in the lives of the patriarchs and matriarchs. Surely Sarah and Rebeccah are depicted in the Torah narrative as strong controlling mothers who exerted great influence on the emerging personas of their sons Isaac and Jacob, the biological and spiritual founders of the emerging Chosen People. The fifth commandment relating to the importance of family life, strikes at the very roots of what was to eventually become the field of psychoanalysis founded by Dr. Sigmund Freud, a descendant of those who stood at Sinai and who heard this commandment.

Coming closer to home and to the consulting room, we find that the boundaries represented by the Decalogue discussed above, have a direct parallel in what psychologists refer to as the conditions of safety for the patient. Before therapy can begin, there already must be in place, a safety structure established by the therapist, such as confidentiality, ability to listen, setting the limits of interaction between patient and therapist, setting of the frame of time and frequency of sessions, etc. Therapists are, in a sense, akin to the role of judges to whom people come for guidance when their own coping mechanisms fail. In effect, the structure of safety for the patient must be in place before the healing work begins following along the same lines as the judicial model set by Jethro in our *Parshah*. Similarly, the boundaries/rules of the Ten Commandments give the Israelites a framework to move on in their psychological development by internalizing these values so they can interact on a more mature level with G-d and man.

Mishpatim
Exodus 21:1-24:18
Civil Legislation

*W*ith the Ten Commandments serving as the foundation of the moral law, the Torah continues on this theme by presenting civil legislation governing social interaction. In this category are a variety of laws concerning: rights of a Hebrew bondsman and bondswoman, personal injuries by man or animal, property damage, murder, theft, moral offenses, sodomy, witchcraft, special consideration for the weak, strangers and even one's enemy, financial dealings and impartiality of justice. There follow laws relating to the new Jewish calendar, specifically the observance of Sabbath, the Three Pilgrimage Festivals and the Sabbatical year. This portion of the weekly Sabbath Torah readings concludes with the people's ratification of the Covenant. Moses reads the Book of the Covenant (Sefer Ha-Brit), and the people respond, "We will do and we will obey." Moses ascends Mt. Sinai for a period of forty days to commune with the Almighty.

Bondage:
An Addiction to Childhood

With the monumental Ten Commandments serving as a base for the moral law, this Parshah proceeds to delineate other boundaries governing interpersonal relationships. In the opening paragraph there is a discussion of what constitutes a bondsman/woman, and what are the respective rights of master and bondsman. The last vestiges of slavery as it was practiced in Egypt are being abolished, as the Torah legislates that servitude is limited, and the servant is not without certain legal rights.

Of specific psychological interest is the Torah's attitude to the slave who chooses to remain with his master after his period of servitude has concluded. He becomes a marked man, literally and figuratively, by having his ear pierced,[1] indicating a blemish in his character. It shows that he is unable to accomplish a basic developmental task, separation, individualization and autonomy (discussed above), which are necessary in becoming a mature individual who can progress on his own. The emotional makeup of this type of personality is one of fixation. According to psychoanalyst P. Blos, "A fixation of drive and ego in the steps of adolescent development is destined to forestall progression into adult personality formation."

---

1. An echo of this ear-piercing practice (and now wearing an earring) is today also a mark of deviation from societal norms, e.g., pirates, hippies in the 60's, gay men, rebellious teenagers, etc.

This fixation, i.e., being stuck, is described by psychoanalyst A. A. Milne in quaint poetic language:

When I was One,
I had just begun.
When I was Two,
I was nearly new.
When I was Three,
I was hardly me.
When I was Four,
I was not much more.
When I was Five,
I was just alive.
When I was Six,
I'm as clever as clever.
So I think I'll be Six,
Forever and ever.

There is a lack of internal harmony in such an individual who is fixated and unable to give up earlier dependency needs. The person who chooses to remain a "slave" may choose many masters to whom he can become subservient, i.e., accumulating wealth, sexual pursuits, addictions, etc.. The wish to remain fixated in a childlike state may not be conscious, but becomes acted out with an externally led master, resulting in a generally empty internal life. Collectively, this is a lesson to the Hebrews that maturation proceeds upon successful completion of developmental tasks. Premature evidence of this maturation process occurred when they responded to the call of Sinai, "We will do and we will listen." This declaration, however, was nothing more than lip service, as they did not listen. In the face of each adversity they regressed to infantile behavior, "*kvetching*," as it is known in Yiddish, and were punished accordingly.

The *Parshah* then proceeds to present a blueprint of rules governing interpersonal relations to establish the parameters that lead to maturity. There follow a series of civil legislation to guide the Israelites in interpersonal relationships; personal injury, property damage, moral offenses, etc. Whereas these rules are experienced at first as external, reinforced by others (judges); the goal, however, being that in the process of their development, they would be internalized to provide a foundation for self-discipline and accepting responsibility for their actions.

This process of internalization is similar to the process of the adolescent in his struggles to learn to control his impulses, and to gradually push away from his parents towards independence. These adolescent struggles eventually lead to one's ability to function as an adult, by learning how to maintain one's self esteem and to accept personal commitment in the face of life's challenges. He has then reached a stage when he is not enslaved to his internal drives or to the dictates of his parents or environment, but is free to be close to his parents while enjoying his independence. This entails one's ability to withdraw "libido" from infantile objects in order to individuate and move on in one's development. In the development of the Israelites, this means detaching from dependence upon the illusory power of Egyptian idols and taskmasters. This dependency is played out now in the new legislation governing the relationship of the slave to his master. The Torah is psychologically prescient in preventing this dependency from happening by denouncing the habitual slave. The slave who chooses to remain enslaved, who has not given up the Egyptian slave mentality, is incapable of entering into the new covenant between a free Israel and G-d, because he has not matured to the point of giving up infantile levels of gratification and dependency. He is fixated in the stage of child dependency and is, therefore, unable to commit to himself or to others as a mature adult. His ear is pierced and rendered defective, because he is psychologically still a child and unable to listen and understand the new mission of the new nation. He may have left Egypt in body, but in spirit he is still enslaved. With the outer trappings of nationhood and governance in place, the Torah now turns to the evolving structure of spiritual life centered around the building of the *Mishkan* (Tabernacle).

Terumah
Exodus 25:1-27:19
Building the Sanctuary

*W*ith Moses ensconced on Mt. Sinai in G-d's presence, the weekly Torah portion shifts to another topic, the building of the Mishkan (Tabernacle). G-d adjures Moses to ask the people to contribute sundry items for building a sanctuary so that G-d's presence would be among them. First, is the description of the Holy Ark which is to contain the two stone tablets. Second, is a description of the table of twelve shewbread. Third, is the Menorah (Candelabrum), consisting of seven lamps. Fourth, is a description of the altar upon which sacrifices are to be offered. The construction of the interior and exterior of the portable Mishkan/Tabernacle is described; curtains supported upon a wooden framework, the outer protective covering of the tabernacle, a veil partitioning the Holy of Holies from the remaining parts of the tabernacle, and the enclosed courtyard marking off the limits of the Sanctuary. All of the above, including the vessels contained therein, their specific dimensions and materials are described in meticulous detail.

Building the
Mishkan (Tabernacle):
A Paradigm for Building Character

This week's Torah portion opens with the following command, "Take for Me an offering [*terumah*] of every man whose heart is willing" (Exod. 19:2) for building a *Mishkan* (Sanctuary/ Tabernacle). It is up to each adult person to make a contribution of his own free will, if he chooses to establish a connection with the G-d of Israel. The Hebrew word *terumah* connotes the concept of "lifting up," as if to indicate that adults are elevated by virtue of their giving towards building the Sanctuary. Children, on the other hand, are accustomed to receiving. It is through the role model of the giving parent that the child learns to progress to a higher stage of maturity upon realizing that giving does not mean depletion. The willingness to give, builds a sense of pleasure in being able to have something to share with others, which builds a sense of gratitude through the act of giving. This allows the child to develop a sense of altruism to be able to give back what was given to him emotionally by his parents. Melanie Klein, a noted psychoanalyst, wrote extensively about the importance of reaching this higher psychological stage of giving as opposed to receiving. Every adult is therefore expected to give a half shekel as a demonstration that each individual has something of value to offer to G-d and to the community. This concept of equality in giving a half shekel implies that the value of each person is not determined by material possessions, but by sharing equally in supporting the new Sanctuary.

This concept of growth and maturity through the act of giving is symbolized by the childlike Cherubim that overarch the Ark of the

Covenant within the *Mishkan*. In fact, this new nation is referred to as *Benei Yisrael*, "Children of Israel," since G-d, the parental figure, provides them with food, water and physical sustenance. As children take from parents, so do the people take from G-d's blessings such as the Manna. In this stage of their development, however, G-d says it is time now to learn to give back to Me and to share with others. While this *Parshah* deals ostensibly with the construction of the Mishkan and its accoutrements, e.g., ark, table of shewbread and altar, it is also a paradigm for building the internal psyche of the individual through the act of giving.

The uncharacteristic detailed Torah description of the minutia of building materials, is also related to the arduous process of building the character of the individual. The fact that this *Parshah* follows the previous two portions of *Mishpatim* and *Jethro*, with their extensive list of civil and religious laws, indicates that both the external and internal developments are interrelated. If one wishes to build a beautiful sanctuary, all of its component parts must mesh together just as the preponderance of civil laws are designed to form a well-functioning society. The emphasis on the quality of material being used, e.g., gold, silver, acacia wood, etc., completes the metaphor that children, *a la* the Cherubim, must receive quality time from each of the parents in order produce the necessary self-esteem for evolving maturity. It is the daily hard work of parenting that helps shape the child's personality in much the same way as the *Mishkan* takes shape due to all the meticulous efforts of the guiding chief architects, Bezalel and Oholiav.

Just as the Cherubim are symbolic of the growth process, similarly the four horn-shaped corners of the *mizbeach* (altar) also have important symbolic value. They are designed to represent the importance of communication. The *shofar* (ram's horn), traditionally marked communication to the people by announcing important events such as a new king's coronation, a New Year, etc. Similarly, the offering of sacrifices on the altar was man's way of communicating with G-d. What better symbolism to represent this interaction than the four *shofar* corners protruding from the *mizbeach*. This communication is another example of the importance of giving back to G-d, through sacrificial offerings of gratitude, for all He has given. The building of the Sanctuary with all its accoutrements is, therefore, providing a model that emotional maturity is displayed by being able to show gratitude in giving back to G-d and to others.

The Holy Ark, located below the overarching Cherubim, is considered to be the most dominant object in the Sanctuary. Its design also conveys an important psychological message. "And thou shalt make an Ark of acacia wood.... And thou shalt overlay it with pure gold within and without shalt thou overlay it..." (Exod. 25:10-11). The Ark was encased within and without in pure gold, but its interior construction was made of wood, representing a living growing object. This wooden interior serves as a metaphor for the growing mechanism of the human psyche, consisting of the id, ego and super ego. It is "housed" in a golden frame, representing parental structure and nurture. The Cherubim, with their outstretched wings above, represent a safe protective holding environment for children to grow and develop. Inside the Holy Ark are the Tablets of the Law, representing the Torah value system and guiding spirituality of G-d which need to be internalized into the human psyche. With the detailed description of the *Mishkan*, when viewed from its metaphoric psychological application in addition to its architectural design, one can begin to appreciate its relevance and importance in building character.

Tetzaveh
Exodus 27:20-30:10
The Priestly Vestments

*T*his portion continues with the theme of the new Sanctuary, focusing on the priests in charge of serving its various functions. Primary was the role of Aaron, the High priest, who with his sons attended to the Menorah (Candelabrum) to keep it burning continually–Ner Tamid. Moses is instructed to organize the making of Aaron's holy vestments which consisted of an ephod (apron), choshen (breastplate) of twelve assorted stones; robe, checkered tunic, turban, sash, forehead plate, miter and linen trousers. The actual making of the above was done by "wise-hearted" craftsmen. Upon their completion, a seven-day ceremony of consecration of Aaron and his sons was conducted. This portion concludes with a summary of the daily sacrifices offered on behalf of the people, as well as with the daily burning of incense on a special golden altar reserved for that purpose.

Costuming
versus Clothing

When I open the door of my consulting room to greet my patient, the first impression of how he or she is doing is determined by a cursory glance at how the person is put together, especially by one's clothing and grooming. This gives me a partial clue as to whether things are in, or off, balance. I may see a consistently well-groomed patient coming in with mismatched clothing, hair or makeup askew, which are indications that something is amiss. The opposite is also true, when someone appears to be too perfectly groomed, not a hair out of place, which may indicate that the patient is rigidly attentive to appearance. This may suggest an over concern for approval by others, or perhaps a sign of rigidity and fear of change. In any event, outer clothing may be indicative of inner psychic reactions which need to be reckoned with. One may therefore question the motivation behind the detailed ornate priestly vestments described in this week's Torah portion *Tetzaveh*, "And you shall make holy garments for Aaron your brother for splendor and beauty" (Exod. 28:2). The Torah describes Aaron's vestments as being made of white and gold, adorned with a hem of purple pomegranates and bells. The pageantry involved in Aaron's approach to the sacrificial service, accompanied by the ringing of these bells, must have deeply impressed the onlookers by its "splendor and beauty." (Perhaps this may be the source for the popular saying, "I will be there with bells on.") From the text it appears that the motivation for wearing the special priestly garb was to call attention of the masses to the exalted position of Aaron the High priest, to evoke a sense of holiness and awe through appealing to their eyes and ears at the elegance of the priestly attire. It must have served as an additional reminder to Aaron of his special responsibility to the priesthood and to the people, and given him a great feeling of self-esteem in his special position of High Priest to the Almighty.

In treating some patients in the religious Jewish community I have discovered a new role for clothing and that is "costuming," which seems to clash with the above description of the priestly attire. Whereas the priestly garb was colorful and distinctive, "costuming" thrives on conformity. This is observed in the current religious fashion, where males are wearing predominantly black hats and dark suits. This type of conformity and uniformity raises a number of questions. Why choose the color black, usually associated with mourning, in contrast to the Biblical choice of white or gold worn by the priests? More disturbing than the sartorial questions are the psychological implications of conformity. Costuming can become a way of gaining acceptance by the group without revealing one's true character and inner feelings. Conformity can be a sign of over attention to externals at the expense of looking inward. This "sea" of black attire is not only an outward display of conformity, but from a psychological perspective, may even be construed as being a reflection of an unconscious internal state of mourning over the loss of individuality and the beauty of diversity. The need to conform often leads to feelings of powerlessness and stagnation, rather than to creativity which is usually the product of having the freedom to be different. Certainly, being different is endemic to the Jewish people, who are distinguished from other nations in being the Chosen people. In fact, we see in this *Parshah*, the principle of difference being emphasized in the ascension of the priestly class within the ranks of the Israelites. Furthermore, the tribe of Levi from whom the priestly clan is descended, is separated from the other tribes, because of its special role in attending to the physical care of the Mishkan. One may therefore question the psychological implications involved in the dominant role that costuming, i.e., conformity is playing in controlling what one wears.

Whereas I have centered my observations on one branch of the Jewish community, this issue of costuming seems to be prevalent in the overall secular community as well. We are well aware of the conformity and imitation of clothing in the general community where the styles of Paris Hilton, Madonna and designer labels are copied *en masse*. With this mass conformity and costuming comes a sense of dependence on outside sources to provide an identity. This is, in many ways, an attempt to overcome the anomie, alienation and loneliness of today's society by having an instant external costume that says, "look at me, I am one of you." This can replace the need to establish meaningful personal relationships. It also raises the question, at what point does one sacrifice personal identity for the sake of outward identification. This trend seems to run counter to the example of the distinctive colorful clothing being instructed to be worn by Aaron and his descendants. In their march toward maturity, the Israelites through the instructions on the priestly garb are given an important lesson on the splendor and beauty of being different.

Ki Tisa
Exodus 30:11-34:35
The Sin of the Golden Calf

*T*his portion opens with the taking of a census which consists of
each male age twenty and over, contributing a silver half shekel
regardless of one's station in life. The proceeds were to be used in support
of the new Sanctuary. Returning again to the theme of the Mishkan,
G-d instructs Moses to make a laver, wherein the newly consecrated
priests were to wash their hands and feet before officiating. The
specific ingredients in making the anointing oil and the holy incense
are detailed. In this context, Bezalel and Oholiav are mentioned as
the chief craftsmen in charge of the entire building operation. In spite
of the importance of the building operation, it is not to supersede the
observance of the Sabbath day of rest which is reemphasized.

At this point, the text returns to the previous narrative which
finds Moses receiving the Ten Commandments written by G-d
upon two stone tablets at the conclusion of his forty day stay on
Mt. Sinai. In the meantime, the people grow impatient waiting for
Moses' return. Aaron tries to delay by asking them to contribute
gold ornaments which are then fashioned into a golden calf to the
delight of the assembled. Upon descending and seeing this decadent
idolatrous scene, Moses becomes enraged, breaks the stone tablets
and destroys the golden calf. Moses successfully intercedes with
G-d on their behalf, while his fellow Levites avenge G-d's wrath
by killing three thousand idol-worshipers. After the reconciliation,
Moses ascends the mountain again to fashion the second set of stone
tablets. After another forty days of intimate communion with the
Deity, he descends to discover his face is radiant, requiring him to
wear a mask when in contact with the people.

The Golden Calf:
A Transitional Object

There are explorations into the emotional impact upon pre-school children who are prematurely dropped off at day care centers. When a young child is prematurely transferred from the care and environment of the mother figure into unfamiliar surroundings, there is often a change in behavior due to the trauma of separation from the security of the caring maternal source. The child may become withdrawn, sulking or subject to other more "acting out" behaviors. The child appears to be in a state of mourning, owing to the abrupt loss of the familiar surroundings, especially from the caring maternal figure.

Freud gives an insightful example of the pre-school child's developmental struggle with the process of separation from the mother. He observed his grandchild playing with a spool of string. The child would throw out the spool and say, "Oh, Oh!" Then he would retract the spool and thread to his hand and say, "Ah, Ah!" This repetitive behavior was seen by Freud as the child's practice in metaphor, of moving away from the mother and then pulling back to the security of the mother after the adventure of short separation. During the growth process, the child can stay away for longer periods of time after being assured that the maternal security is always available. In this process which continues through much of the child's early development, one begins to internalize the safety and security of the maternal figure. There are times when this process is not completed. The child may then use a transitional object for comfort. This can be a stuffed toy, a piece of a favorite blanket or one's thumb. The more complete the process of individuation, the less need for these transitional objects. Generally, when children have accomplished this phase, they are able to enjoy the separation required in order to go to school.

In this *Parshah, Ki Tisa*, the Israelites, in a sense, behave very much like the above prematurely displaced children, especially the "acting out" ones. Their sudden dramatic exodus, led by a former Egyptian prince at the behest of an unseen G-d-father figure, added to their feelings of displacement and lack of security. The Israelites left Egypt suddenly in a semi-traumatized state leaving all familiar things behind. The sequence of rebellions in the desert is an expression of regression, not unlike the behavior of children who are torn away prematurely from their familiar home environment. Moses' disappearance for forty days, therefore, causes extreme separation anxiety. The two primary causes for this trauma, a new strange hostile environment, and the loss of the single guiding parental figure that Moses provided, prepares the groundwork for regression by making a transitional object, a golden calf reminiscent of Egypt. The people feel lost and helpless. It appears that Aaron is sensitive to this feeling of helplessness, by giving them something to do that would distract them and help them rebound from their helplessness. Aaron's strategy is to provide the grieving "children" with a transitional object as a kind of security blanket to hold on to during the parental figure's (Moses) absence. Aaron's choice of making an idol of a nurturing calf, a familiar Egyptian symbol, is a failed attempt to heal the trauma of loss and separation. Being able to visually see a "god" leader to take Moses' place, in some sense is similar to the failed attempt of showing a child a picture of the mother during the mother's absence to soothe the grieving child.

The symbolism of the calf may represent their own state of being young and helpless, as well as representing the missing nurturing life-giving parent. In his attempt to comfort the people, Aaron provides them with an activity to assuage their separation anxiety. Their dancing and singing around the golden calf, is probably an expression of their joy in feeling powerful enough to recreate the return of the lost "parental" nurturing figure.

Winnicott, a pediatric psychoanalyst, explains the psychological dynamics of how a transitional object allows the infant to begin to withdraw from feeling merged with the nurturing mother into becoming a separate being. When the mother figure is absent for an extended period, the internal memory begins to fade, allowing this withdrawal to happen. In terms of the people's relationship to Moses, the nurturing parental figure, his extended absence left an opening to find a replacement for the internalized lost object. This replacement is the god figure representing mother Egypt symbolized by the nurturing golden calf. The donated golden objects were an unconscious attempt of the people to reinstate this merger, by feeling that "part of me is now part of you." The golden calf helps psychologically to stem their anxiety experienced from the feared abandonment by Moses.

One is, however, still struck why Aaron would choose idolatry as a transitional object, which is the very antithesis of monotheism. Moreover, why would Aaron step in to a leadership role and orchestrate a ceremony so completely alien to everything Moses had taught the people? Is it not possible that Moses' absence stirred up feelings of sibling rivalry in the older brother Aaron against the younger more powerful G-d-favored brother? There were obviously other transitional objects to help the people cope with separation anxiety, so we might be suspicious of Aaron's personal motive in coping with this rebellion.

The return of Moses, despite his anger and disappointment, provides the people with the security of being reunited with their lost nurturing parental figure. Moses' argument with G-d in attempting to rationalize the people's errant behavior, "they are a stiff-necked people," is interpreted as their being obstinate. Obstinacy, in psychological terminology, is a form of resistance to change. This is, in effect, Moses' way of excusing their lapse into idolatry. They are an *am keshe oref*, an obstinate people who are fearful and resistant to change. This entire episode of the golden calf therefore becomes a working through, or a form of collective therapy not unlike the dynamics of treatment of patients who are suffering from separation and loss. Subsequent rebellions are a continuation of this "acting out" process of working through their resistance to change and loss of security, which are an expression of their angry feelings of being displaced from their Egyptian roots.

A deeper psychoanalytic insight into understanding this episode of the golden calf and subsequent rebellions may be derived from the research of the psychoanalyst Ana Maria Rizzuto, who tracked the various stages in the process of developing faith. It begins with the quality of the parental role which fuels the developmental process, both psychologically and religiously. The internalized parental image becomes the anchor upon which the process of faith in G-d is developed. When this anchor is not present, such as when parents are unable to provide the kind of security that allows for separation and individuation, then this process of faith development may become arrested. Similarly now with the Israelites, despite standing at Sinai and escaping the ten plagues, all manifestations of G-d's power, they are still easily seduced by a visible golden calf crafted by humans. This all hearkens back to the people's lack of readiness to accept the belief in an invisible G-d figure. This ability to abstract represents a higher stage of psychological and intellectual development for which the Israelites are obviously not prepared. They have not reached this more sophisticated level of faith as demonstrated in Rizzuto's faith developmental schema. They are akin to our nursery age children discussed above, having been torn away from their maternal source, Egypt, and left to languish in a foreboding wilderness. Lacking the orderly developmental processes needed in building faith, such as demonstrated by Rizzuto's research, they resort to "acting out" in the form of rebellions and regressive behavior. It will take forty years for the Egyptian born parents to perish in the wilderness, so that the new generation nurtured by Moses can develop a faith concept and belief in an unseen G-d. The rebellions, therefore, were not totally negative. When viewed from a psychological perspective, they were, in a sense, necessary in order to work through this transitional period so that the Children of Israel could accept their more mature role as G-d's chosen people.

Vayakhel-Pekudei
Exodus 35:1-38:20 / Exodus 38:21-40:38
Completion of the Tabernacle

*W*hereas the previous portions record the instructions for building the Mishkan, these last two portions in the Book of Exodus deal with the implementation of those instructions: the actual construction of the Tabernacle. The generous contributions of the people of gold, silver, skins, yarns, etc., exceed what is needed. Moses, with the help of the chief craftsmen, Bezalel and Oholiav, surveys the completed Mishkan and declares that it is done just as G-d commanded and he blesses the people. G-d instructs Moses to erect the Mishkan on the first day of the month of Nisan. On that occasion a cloud descends upon the newly completed Mishkan so that the people can feel the glory and presence of the Lord. The Book of Exodus concludes by repeating that the people are guided throughout their journeys by a cloud during the day and a pillar of fire at night.

When is
Enough *Enough?*

Among the many talents Moses exhibits as a leader in uniting a recalcitrant people, is his role as a vocational counselor. (Jacob played a similar role in *Parshat Vayechi.)* This may account in part for the repetition in these last two portions in the book of Exodus, of building instructions of the Sanctuary stated previously in the portions of *Terumah* and *Tetzaveh*. He wishes to emphasize in the building of the *Mishkan*, a new work ethic for the former Egyptian slaves. The first rule in the work place is to recognize that you can only work six days a week. "Six days shall work be done, but on the seventh day there shall be to you a holy day, a Sabbath of solemn rest to the Lord" (Exod. 35:2). The second rule is to recognize that a successful work force requires a division of labor based on a person's skills, "And let every 'wise-hearted' man among you, come and make all that the Lord has commanded" (Exod. 25:10). In Bible terminology, the heart is usually viewed as the seat of intellect. In using the expression "wise-hearted" in reference to work, implies that choosing a vocation involves an internal quest. You have to know yourself, to be introspective, in order to be wise enough to embark on choosing your livelihood. This means to search your "heart" in order to be able to determine your abilities and talents and act accordingly. No one is commanded to choose a particular occupation because it would please one's parents. Moses is teaching the people that choosing a line of work is no longer arbitrary a la slavery, but is an internal process involving the confluence of heart and mind "wise-hearted." The third rule in the work place is the importance of adhering to the detailed instructions set in building the Mishkan. Exactitude in following instructions is what is emphasized repeatedly in building the Mishkan, and all of its appurtenances e.g. the altar, art, candelabrum, etc.

The Torah then records a remarkable response on the part of the people at the conclusion of this entire building project. "The people bring much more than enough for the service of the work which the Lord commanded them to make. And Moses commanded ... 'Let neither man nor woman make any more work for the offering of the Sanctuary.' So the people were restrained from bringing. For the stuff they had was sufficient for all the work to make it, and too much" (Exod. 36:5-7). Moses is teaching the people the concept of what is "enough." Boundaries are being set based on the concept of what constitutes enough. Accordingly, the Torah goes to great lengths (four *Parshiyot*) to spell out how much is enough in order to build the *Mishkan*. Over-giving can be just as destructive as under-giving, a lesson that affluent parents of privileged children have lamentably learned.

In the consulting room, I meet patients who struggle with excesses, and yet continue to feel deprived and empty inside. Their inner structure of limits, i.e., enough, has not been properly developed. When Moses said, "for the stuff they had was sufficient," he implied that men and women with "hearts of wisdom" realize when that point has been reached. Enough is a feeling of internal satisfaction, and a feeling of fullness which is capable of taming greed. In *Pirkei Avot*, "Ethics of the Fathers," this understanding is expressed in the pithy saying, "Who is rich, one who is happy with his lot." Weight problems, for example, are often a result of an attempt to use external food as a substitute for an inner feeling of emptiness and as a means to repair feelings of internal deprivation.

The design of the *Mishkan* is, therefore, not just an architectural blueprint, but a metaphor for human behavior. Those who are wise-hearted are the ones who can both feel *lev* (heart), and "understand" (*hacham*) the many psychological insights embedded in this physical edifice. There are limitations and parameters within which the concept of enough is transmitted. There is only one Sabbath a week, not two. The holy ark containing the *luhot* (Ten Commandments) is to be two and a half (2 ½) *ammot* wide, not three, and so on with all the work and materials in the building of the *Mishkan*. The repetition of the phrase "each as they are willing" gives the people the option of participating in this effort, something they could not do as slaves in Egypt. This vocational choice, however, comes with accepting responsibility which is made possible by their new found freedom. This responsibility entails adhering to the various building instructions designed to spell out the definition of what is sufficient. At the conclusion of this project the Torah records, "according to all that the Lord commanded Moses, so the children of Israel did all the work. And Moses saw all the work, and behold they had done it; as the Lord had commanded, even so they had done it. And Blessed them" (Exod. 39:42). This concluding statement implies their reaching a more mature level of growth both individually and collectively as a nation.

As we come to the end of the book of Exodus, we begin to see a similarity between the building of the *Mishkan*, as representing the psychological as well as physical development of the Jewish people, and the opening chapter of the Book of Genesis. In the opening chapter, G-d creates boundaries and separation between land and sea, and G-d said, "It was good." Then there was the establishment of light and darkness which provides discreet boundaries of time, and subsequent separation into days of the week. The completion of the task of creation was the institution of the Sabbath, following the creation of man. Discreet boundaries, the management of time and the ability to separate and say enough, are part of G-d's design for man to follow. G-d gives us an opportunity in the building of the *Mishkan*, to repeat these same steps as was taken in His creation of the universe. The maturation process allows people to develop discrete boundaries, to manage time, to know how to work, to collaborate and to manage their infantile greed by being able to follow G-d's command to be satisfied when enough is enough. This understanding underlies the connection between G-d's design of creation in the opening chapter in Genesis, and this closing chapter in Exodus.

We also now begin to see retrospectively, the changes in the Children of Israel progressing from a stage of slave mentality to a more mature stage of freedom which allows them the opportunity of making choices, but with the added responsibility of carrying them out. In the end, the Torah affirms their successful completion of this monumental undertaking. "And behold they had done it as the Lord commanded even so they had done it. And G-d blessed them." The blessing may very well be their building of an internal sense of power and accomplishment which they could never have experienced as slaves in Egypt.

THE BOOK OF LEVITICUS

"And the Lord called unto Moses and spoke unto him... 'When
any man of you bringeth an offering unto the Lord...'"
— *Leviticus* 1:1-2

Vayikra
Leviticus 1:1-5:26
The Laws of Sacrifice

*T*his Parshah, as well as much of the book of Leviticus, deals
with the laws of the priests who are an off shoot of the tribe of
Levi, hence the Latin name, Leviticus. It begins by discussing the
various sacrifices brought in the Mishkan, the Tabernacle. The first
animal sacrifice described is the Olah, the burnt offering, which
as its Hebrew name indicates was completely consumed in fire on
the altar. Another form of offering is the Minhah, a meal offering
consisting of flour, oil and frankincense. The priests receive a portion
of this offering, while the rest is burned on the altar. Another type of
animal sacrifice is the Shelamim, peace offering, which is shared by
its offerer and his guests. Guilt offerings are designated for various
inadvertent sins, transgressions, ritual impurity, misusing sanctified
property, dishonesty, breach of trust, etc. The Torah also prohibits
the consumption of blood and certain animal fats. These offerings
(where applicable) are accompanied by verbal confessions of the sins
committed, placing of the hand upon the animal sacrifice and in
civil matters, making full restitution to any aggrieved individual.

Psychological Implications in the Sacrificial Rituals

L eviticus, the third book of the Pentateuch, opens with a discussion of priestly duties conducted in the newly constructed *Mishkan* (tabernacle), which was described in detail at the end of the book of Exodus. Underlying these duties is the basic religious principle of maintaining holiness and purity. As discussed above, separation and individuation are part of G-d's design to preserve this sense of holiness within the new Israelite nation. This design operates both externally, in Israel's separation from the surrounding nations, and internally, within its own people.

The tribe of Levi, from whom the Latin name for the Book of Leviticus is derived, is separated from the other tribes in being responsible for the physical care of the *Mishkan*. The officiants who conduct the rituals in the *Mishkan*, especially the offering of sacrifices, are from the priestly clan headed by Aaron, the high priest. The priestly clan represents a further separation in being an off shoot of the tribe of Levi, which tribe is endowed with the highest degree of holiness.

Within this framework of holiness, the book of Leviticus spells out the specific duties to be performed by Aaron and his family. Here too, as was noted above in the building of the *Mishkan* and its holy vessels, the Torah incorporates certain subtle psychological insights into what appears to be rote physical rituals. While not described as such in Biblical terminology, these psychological nuances are nevertheless present in these sacrificial rituals. For example, in the very beginning of this week's Torah portion, *Vayikra*, we read, "And he [the offerer of the sacrifice] shall lay his hand upon the head of the burnt offering, and it shall be accepted for him [by the priest] to make atonement for him" (Lev. 1:4).

This act the of laying on of hands was accompanied with some type of confession depending on the type of sacrifice being offered. The Torah, therefore, recognizes that these sacrificial rituals involve a twofold process: offering up a sacrifice (external), and making a personal confession (internal). The supplicant must recognize and articulate what he has done wrong, and brings a sacrifice as a form of restitution restoring his relationship with G-d. The laying on of hands upon the animal's head symbolizes his admission of guilt; it is tantamount to declaring, "I transfer the sin I have committed unto this animal/scapegoat in order that I shall be relieved of the guilt which I bear."

Guilt arises when a person recognizes he has done something wrong by violating an ethical, moral or religious principle. Often, such realization is accompanied by lowered self-esteem and increased anxiety. In psychological terms, this is the anxiety experienced by the ego when confronted by the super ego (conscience). The ego feels something terrible will happen within the psychic system. That is, certain essentials of life such as love, well-being and security will be cut off. Cognizant that we are all apt to sin, whether deliberately or unwittingly, the Torah provides a remedy in the form of a ritual sacrifice to assuage the guilt. The sacrifice offers the opportunity for the penitent to attain closure regarding the sin, rather than remaining overly self-punitive and guilt-ridden. In this way the individual can be self-forgiving and also be forgiven by G-d. This process of repentance and restitution paves the way for continued personal growth and restoring one's self-esteem.

One often encounters in the consulting room, clients who feel they have no options other than continuing to repeat a pattern of futile behavior that yields only feelings of guilt, inferiority and failure. This Torah portion, which deals ostensibly with the rituals of sacrifice, in fact presents a psychological formula for ridding oneself of unresolved guilt. The laying on of hands and confession provide a kind of ritual which says, "I have performed the requirements for correction of my errant behavior, and I am now free to go forward in my personal growth."

In addition to redressing of sin and resolution of guilt, the sacrificial ritual also emphasizes one's need for relationships with others. We are not alone in our anguish. The sacrificial rituals involve association with priests. This reduces our narcissistic tendency for self-deception in our belief that we do not need others. Whether the other is human, or the All Powerful, Forgiving Father, we are all dependent on one another. This reflects the Torah's intuitive perceptiveness of the human condition, especially of a psychological nature, because it provides a variety of means of coping with internal issues.

Taking the offering of sacrifices a step further in its psychological implications, we note, "If his offering be a burnt offering of the herd, he shall offer it a male without blemish…" (Lev. 1:3). The choosing of an unblemished animal for expiating sin creates a necessary burden on the sinner to sacrifice something of much material value. This drives home the lesson that ridding oneself of sin and guilt is "serious business," materially as well as emotionally. The imagery of the rising sacrificial smoke serves as a powerful symbol and metaphor for the expiation and disappearance of sin.

The bulk of this week's Torah reading deals with ritual sins committed between man and G-d, involving such matters as ritual impurity, violating religious vows, etc. In this context, the Torah appears to be highly mechanical and prescriptive. This is, however, not unlike the rituals associated with many professions. In psychoanalysis, for example, there are also rituals, such as the analyst opening and closing the door for the patient. The analyst is seated behind the patient taking notes, while the patient free associates in a comfortable supine position on the couch. The patient always begins the dialogue, not the analyst. These, as well as other procedures have psychological explanations, yet must be adhered to in the manner described, not unlike what has been discussed above with regard to sacrificial rituals. These rituals based on repetitive behavior produce a feeling of safety within their respective settings.

Some of the rituals described above, in the offering of sacrifices, are practiced today in traditional Jewish homes. The altar upon which sacrifices were offered is represented today by one's dining table. On the Sabbath, for example, the two *Hallah* loaves are salted in commemoration of a similar practice associated with the offering of sacrifices. Of related interest are the many rules observed today that accompany the eating of food. The observance of these rules/rituals is an essential part of social etiquette, and of "good table manners." These are reminiscent of what is being prescribed in this week's Torah reading relating to the many sacrificial rituals.

These sacrificial rituals incorporate a variety of psychological implications. For example, the ritual slaughtering of the animal, served as an outlet for a person's feelings of aggression. The ritual of laying of hands on the animal as mentioned above, elicited feelings of remorse for some moral offense, since an innocent creature was being symbolically offered in his stead. Watching the priest perform the various ritual ceremonials was not only an impressive visual experience, but was an important means of developing respect for authority which would hopefully mature into self-discipline. This ritual orientation emphasized throughout the book of Leviticus, becomes the proving ground for Israel's further development of structure and commitment to a religiously oriented lifestyle as well as fostering their continued psychological growth.

Tzav
Leviticus 6:1-8:36
Instructions to the Priests

Whereas the previous Parshah was addressed to the Children of Israel, this Parshah is specifically addressed to the Priests. It discusses the Korban Tamid (perpetual offering) brought daily in the morning and afternoon, for which the fire on the altar must be kept burning continuously. The daily special offering of the Kohen Gadol (high priest) is discussed. Details concerning the Hattat (involuntary transgression), Asham (guilt), Shelamim (peace) and Todah (thanksgiving) offerings are presented. Time limits are given governing when certain sacrifices may be eaten, after which they are to be burned. One who is ritually impure may not partake of these sacrifices. The Parshah ends with the consecration of Aaron and his sons, and the inauguration of the Mishkan service.

Ritual Sacrifices and
the Process of Human Development

Although there have been various theological explanations for the institution of animal sacrifices, I would like to add a psychological explanation of how sacrifices provide an avenue for human growth. In early childhood, the child receives the foundation for security and self-esteem, by being taken care of through family structure, personal safety and maternal caring. The child, who is adequately nurtured, internalizes the image of the good mother. This internalized feeling of goodness and bounty allows the child to feel loved and lovable, to be alone yet not lonely. The child receives this nurture with a sense of entitlement. Initially the child views the caregiver and the giving, as part of oneself and one's own omnipotence. In the process of receiving nurture, growth gradually proceeds to a point when the door begins to open towards separation and autonomy.

This opening also involves learning what it means to sacrifice, by giving up some of one's "creature comforts." The child gives up certain freedoms and animalistic behavior by "sacrificing" these freedoms in exchange for the love of his parents. One of the earliest of these sacrifices is toilet training, when the child gives up his right to gratify his bodily functions without restriction. The child also sacrifices elements of greed by learning to share his toys with others. He must learn to curb his aggression and desire to destroy in order to be part of a family. These steps represent the initial stages in developing the ability to sacrifice for the greater good. The child can now derive satisfaction by giving, as the internalized maternal image had given to him.

Having learned how to sacrifice, the child can then differentiate between being a receiver and becoming a giver to others. With this basis of being given to, and eventually giving up this sense of entitlement, he begins to appreciate the benefits and generosity of becoming the giver. Psychoanalyst Melanie Klein considers the child's ability to develop gratitude as a distinct step in his developmental progress. However, those who have not been nurtured sufficiently often feel unworthy of receiving; those are the ones who have not reached the mature stage of expressing gratitude and of being able to give to others.

Offering of religious sacrifices to G-d is the Biblical way of developing this process of human growth, culminating in one's ability to express gratitude by giving to others. Recent research by Robert Emmons and Michael McCullough has shown that the ability to express gratitude has powerful consequences for healthy well-being and altruistic behavior. For example, individuals who attend services regularly and engage in religious activities were found to be more likely to express gratitude in life situations. Grateful people are more likely to believe in the interconnectedness of life, to respect others and to commit themselves to relationships. They also report that such individuals possess greater optimism and vitality, and suffer less from depression. Today, when we no longer offer sacrifices, gratitude is commonly expressed by the institution of giving charity, doing good deeds and working for good causes to improve the world (*Tikkun Olam*).

This *Parshah*, *Tzav* (Command), enumerates various types of sacrificial offerings associated with errant religious behavior. The *Olah*, *Hattat* and *Asham* are generally sacrifices by which one derives expiation and forgiveness for sins in violation of religious law. Yet, because the supplicant expects to receive full forgiveness, psychologically he is still considered to be a recipient. A higher level of emotional maturity is expressed by the Todah (thanksgiving) offering, the most altruistic of all the sacrifices, because the person expresses thanks for some good fortune without expecting anything in return. The various sacrifices enumerated in this *Parshah* serve not only as controls over errant behavior, but constitute an important training ground for the Israelites in cultivating a sense of responsibility, commitment and gratitude.

Although the entire sacrificial service presided over by the *Kohanim* (Priests) has ceased, the introduction of prayer has enabled worshipers to express feelings similar to those evoked by the animal sacrifices. Since the destruction of the Second Temple in 70 C.E., prayer has been substituted for animal sacrifices. In memory of the sacrificial services, prayer is recited facing Jerusalem, toward the site of the ancient Temple. Prayer is now regarded as *avodat ha-lev* (service of the heart) in lieu of offering physical sacrifices. The Hebrew word for sacrifice is *korban*, from the root meaning "near," since the object of bringing a *korban* was to draw oneself nearer to G-d. In this way, humans begin to realize their limitations and mortality. Through prayer, the sacrificial substitute, one may contemplate one's shortcomings and mortality and draw ever nearer to the Source of all blessing. The Children of Israel in this early stage of nationhood, are learning through the instructions on the sacrificial service, how to develop the inner resources needed to be able to reach out to a Higher Being and hopefully to others as well.

Shemini
Leviticus 9:1-11:47
Consecration of the Priests

This Parshah opens with a description of the various offerings made on the eighth (Shemini) day of the consecration of Aaron and his sons into the Sanctuary service. This momentous happy occasion is marred by the tragic, sudden death of Nadav and Avihu, two of the four sons of Aaron. The Torah attributes their death to "bringing a strange fire before the Lord, which He had not commanded them." Aaron is dumbstruck and is consoled by his brother Moses. The priests are warned never to drink intoxicating beverages before engaging in their service in the Sanctuary. The Torah then discusses laws of ritual purity, centering on the dietary laws. Kosher animals are those that have both cloven hooves and chew their cud. Kosher fish are those that also have two characteristics; fins and removable scales. The Parshah enumerates all birds and fowl that are forbidden, which generally fall into the category of birds of prey. It then enumerates various criteria to identify fowl which may be eaten. All types of insects are forbidden to be eaten, except for certain species of locusts. Certain dead species cause ritual impurity upon contact, requiring a purification process. The Parshah summarizes its emphasis upon ritual purity by admonishing Israel to be holy and separate for "I am Holy."

Strange Fire:
The Hidden Role of the Unconscious

One of the major subjects that is discussed in this week's Torah reading, *Shemini* (eighth), is the sudden and tragic deaths of Nadav and Avihu, sons of the high priest Aaron. The cause given for their deaths is, however, ambiguous, "They brought a strange fire that G-d did not command" (Lev. 10:1). The Bible commentators are divided over how to interpret this "strange fire", whether in a positive light (they were overzealous) or negative (impetuous rebellious youth). When analyzed from a psychological perspective, however, this action of Aaron's two sons has a deeper unconscious motive.

First, we need to look at the context surrounding this tragic episode. Aaron is being inducted into the exalted position of becoming the first high priest of Israel. He becomes the quintessential role model of a father to his four sons. Yet we know that children very often pick up unconscious attitudes that lie beneath the surface of outward behavior. In the case of Aaron, we read previously about his role in indirectly engineering a serious infraction of monotheism by firing up a molten golden calf thereby bringing a strange (idolatrous) fire into the camp.

There are various opinions as to what motivated Aaron's collusion with the people in fashioning the golden calf. Could it be that it stemmed from his unconscious desire to unseat his younger brother in the power structure and to become the favored one among the people? Moses has not returned from the mountain, it therefore devolves upon Aaron to take over. After all, being the older brother, he was slated to be in the main leadership position in the family. This is a throw-back to the unresolved sibling rivalries that wreaked havoc in the patriarchal families. Similarly here, it is only natural that the more articulate Aaron would harbor unconscious feelings of sibling rivalry toward his younger brother.

This helps explain why Nadav and Avihu chose a "strange fire" as the symbol of their rebellion. It is modeled after their father Aaron's using fire to forge the golden calf in defiance of everything that Moses and G-d stood for. We might, therefore, question what kind of unconscious role model Aaron really served to his sons from this episode in spite of all the regal splendor of the high priesthood. Nadav and Avihu picked up the unconscious message that one does not always have to follow the voice of authority, but can, under certain conditions, "take the law into his own hands." Moreover, the use of fire in both instances of rebellion is in keeping with Freud's view on the symbolism of fire. It signifies feelings of anger, aggression and rebellion. All of these emotions are involved in these episodes.

This identification of the child with the unconscious message of parents is a common phenomenon in all social classes. A well-to-do father who is a professional, came to seek my counsel ostensibly concerning his delinquent son. Little did he realize that his perceptive son picked up his father's own hidden delinquencies in reporting taxes, in business dealings and abuses in family relationships. We are often uncomfortable with how perceptive our children are in reading between the lines of our outward behavior. We know that so much of our conscious life is driven by our unconscious desires that we may not be so willing to see and acknowledge their existence. This *Parshah* is an example of hidden fiery aggressive power issues that are not resolved. Being the priestly first family and serving as role models for the rest of the people, Aaron's sons were guilty of a very serious infraction and were punished accordingly, "And Aaron was silent" (Lev. 10:3), a silent unconscious testimony of deep-seated guilt and internal suffering over his role in the golden calf apostasy which was apparently not lost on these two sons.

Tazria
Leviticus 12:1-13:59
Laws of Purification

*C*ontinuing its discussion of ritual purity, this Parshah distinguishes the purification process for the childbearing mother, depending on whether she gives birth to a male or female child. It then discusses the diagnosis and treatment of one who suffers from leprosy. It discusses in great detail the symptoms of the disease which may afflict one's clothing as well as one's body. The person who is afflicted with this disease is to consult with a priest who will then guide him in the intricate purification process.

Gender Differences are O.K., Inequality is Not

This *Parshah*, *Tazria*, in discussing the issue of ritual impurity of the mother during the birthing process, emphasizes the differences between the genders. They are separate and different, but are not necessarily unequal. Sexual differences must be acknowledged in order for the genders to perform their biologically separate roles. In fact, these gender differences are essential in maintaining G-d's design of *Kedushah* which is built upon the premise of being separate and different.

This principle of *Kedushah* helps explain what on the surface appears to present a moral dilemma. The Torah states in the opening of this *Parshah*, "If a woman be delivered and bears a male child, then she shall be unclean seven days... but if she bears a female child, then she shall be unclean two weeks..." (Lev. 12:2, 5). Why is the total period of ritual impurity for the mother—fourteen days, when giving birth to a daughter, whereas only seven days when delivering a son? The explanation, which I draw from psychology rather than theology, involves an insight into the psyche of the expectant father in Biblical times. A male heir is preferred, because he will become the breadwinner in the family as well as insuring the father's immortality. The family name is transmitted by the male heir not by the female. Giving birth to a daughter means incurring an additional financial responsibility, culminating in providing a generous dowry upon her marriage. The Torah, sensitive to this reality, legislates a longer (fourteen day) "cooling off " period for the expectant father to overcome his disappointment in not having a son, as well as assuaging his unconscious anger towards his wife, so they can then resume conjugal relations. This is not the case when delivering a son, a productive male heir; therefore the period of the mother's ritual impurity is cut in half (seven days).

Helena Deutch, a psychoanalyst who has written extensively on the psychology of women, deals with some of the physical and psychological changes occurring in women following childbirth. She contends that if for any reason the mother feels the husband's withdrawal or anger following childbirth, this can set the stage for a post-partum depressive reaction. The physical act of giving birth carries with it a mother's feelings of loss and separation from the living organism that was within her. When this loss is compounded by her husband's disappointment of fathering a girl, it is not unusual for her to feel apprehensive, and need more time to adjust. Similarly, it will be difficult for her husband to hide his disappointment. This longer "cooling off " period gives both husband and wife the "space" necessary before resuming intimate relations. It turns out that here again the Torah is prescient in anticipating the psychological needs of husband and wife at such a crucial, trying period in marital relations.

This difference between the genders, however, does not translate into inequality. After the period of the mother's purification is completed, the Torah states, "...and when the days of her purification are fulfilled, for a son, or for a daughter, she shall bring a lamb of the first year for a burnt offering and a young pigeon or turtle dove, for a sin offering unto the door of the tent of meeting, unto the priest" (Lev. 12:6).

The offering of purity brought by the mother is uniform whether giving birth to a male or female, emphasizing that when the birthing ordeal is over, the offering restores the basic principle of equal status between the sexes. Considering the times in which the Bible was written, this principle is indeed visionary. This is an important milestone in defining the relationship between the genders as well as in the Torah's insight into the unconscious workings of the minds of the sexes.

When childbirth is also viewed from the perspective of *Kedushah*, this is another example where differences and separation are acknowledged and encouraged in Judaism. The Torah in this Parshah is providing an important lesson in how to handle gender differences, and that implicitly, psychological emotional considerations must be reckoned with in legislating relationships between husband and wife.

Metzora
Leviticus 14:1-15:33
Purification of a Leper

*T*his Parshah continues its discussion of the Metzora (Leper), by further describing the purification process which concludes with his bringing sacrifices and immersion in a Mikveh (a ritual pool). The Parshah then describes the purification process involved when leprosy afflicts one's residence. The Parshah concludes its discussion of ritual impurity by detailing various physical secretions which render a person unclean, thereby preventing contact with anything that is sanctified. The cleansing process and its duration is discussed, especially the important role played by the priest in this entire process.

The Walls have Ears: Ramifications of Evil Talk

This *Parshah*, *Metzora* (leper), deals with the diagnosis and treatment of a physical affliction translated as leprosy, a deteriorating disease of the skin. The Midrash, however, views this disease not only as a physical malady, but as a spiritual one, owing its inception to *lashon hara* (evil talk/tale-bearing). This Midrashic interpretation is derived from the Hebrew title *Metzora*, which can be divided into two separate words *motzi ra* (uttering evil talk). Because this disease was viewed as contagious, the leper was dispatched outside of the camp. When deemed cured of this malady by a priest, the afflicted could return to the camp after an involved purification process which concluded with guilt/sin offerings. It appears that in the isolation and bringing of these sacrifices, the Midrash is alluding to what is recognized today in medical science as the mind–body connection. In other words, the leper's physical condition is caused by a moral offense, that of evil talk concerning others.

Paramount in the purification process of the leper is his dependence upon the *Kohen* (priest) healer. The *Kohen* serves as the ersatz physician in the diagnosis and in determining when the leper is cured. The leper can presumably relate better to a *Kohen*, who is also a "loner" separated from others by virtue of his special religious status. He is, therefore, better able to serve as a role model not only in treating the leper's physical condition, but in treating his moral character as well. Of special interest in this inter-relationship is the fact that the *Kohen*, like the *Metzora*, may also suffer from a characterological flaw. According to Talmudic sources the priests were known as *kapdanim*. That is, they were subject to "volatile anger." However, the Torah in its inimitable way provides positive avenues of displacing this inherent anger through various rituals associated with offering animal sacrifices, e.g., slaughtering, sprinkling the blood, flaying the hide, burning, etc. The *Metzora*, however, who resorts to *lashon hara* (evil talk), finds his psychological outlet in inappropriate ways by slandering others. This becomes his external diversion from looking inward to his own psychological deficits consisting of feelings of envy and inferiority. This inappropriate coping mechanism becomes self-defeating, since the mind-body connection is telling him the truth through its eruption of skin lesions. Therefore, he is distanced from others and sent outside the camp, where the sympathetic priest not only ministers to his physical condition, but also to his psyche.

This intimate collaboration between the penitent and the *Kohen* in the purification process is a prescient insight of the Midrash into what is today recognized as the patient-therapist relationship. More and more I am seeing patients referred to me by internists who ostensibly are treating physical maladies such as migraines, high blood pressure, ulcers, eating disorders, etc. The more astute physicians are realizing that in treating these physical conditions one must also reckon with the emotional stresses which are often causes for these illnesses. The Midrash, thousands of years ago, intuited that the leper's skin disease had a psychological/emotional etiology which also needed to be treated. Research in the mind-body connection was conducted in the 1950s by Franz Alexander, a past director of the Chicago Institute of Psychoanalysis. A cogent example of one of his findings was that skin eruptions, such as oozing sores, may be physical manifestations of unrecognized internal weeping. The American Institute on Stress estimates that as many as 70% to 90% of visits to health care providers result from some form of stress disorder. Since skin is the largest organ in the body, it is most susceptible to internal stress reactions.

This is ample confirmation of the Midrashic assertion that skin disorders e.g. leprosy could very well be related to an individual's need to malign others, *lashon hara*, due to anger, envy or other internal issues.

One can, however, challenge this Midrashic interpretation of the leper by pointing to the fact that the leprosy "virus" not only afflicts humans, but even physical structures. We read, "When ye come into the land of Canaan which I give to you for a possession, and I put the plague of leprosy in a house…the priest shall go in to see the house…" (Lev. 14:34-35). From this, one would be inclined to regard leprosy as caused by some kind of fungus which corrodes the physical structure. How can *lashon hara* (evil talk) corrode the walls of a person's home? Nevertheless, the Midrash could counter this argument by showing that evil talk can afflict the surrounding environment as well as the person. The inspection of the person's dwelling by the *Kohen* is not only to search for bacteria in the walls, but is an allusion to the subtle negative psychological impact tale bearing can have upon the entire household. The expression, "the walls have ears" affirms this concept, especially when children hear parents constantly maligning others. The fact that the Midrash is so sensitive to the physical and spiritual effects of evil talk and to its "side effects" is most instructive. It paves the way for a better understanding of the mind-body connection and the interfacing of medical science with religious life.

Aharei Mot
Leviticus 16:1-18:30
Instituting the Day of Atonement

*T*his Parshah begins by harking back to the tragic death (Aharei
Mot) of Aaron's two sons, and by cautioning Aaron to be
extremely careful whenever he enters the Mishkan. Aaron is then
instructed about all the awesome rituals he is to perform on Yom
Kippur (Day of Atonement), the offerings he is to bring, changing of
his attire and his purification process. Central to these atonement
rituals is the selection by lottery of two goats, one is offered on
Aaron's behalf and on behalf of his priestly family, and the other is
designated a "scapegoat," bearing the sins of all the people. It is then
driven into the wilderness. Yom Kippur is designated as a day that
"ye shall afflict your souls" (fasting), which is to occur annually on
the tenth day of the seventh month in the lunar calendar. Animals
and fowl intended for sacrifices could only be offered in the Mishkan
in accordance with detailed instructions. Consumption of blood
is forbidden. The Parshah concludes by enumerating forbidden
incestuous marriages, homosexuality, being unchaste, human
sacrifices and other types of perversions. These are all considered
abominations that defile the person and subject him to severe
punishment, "for I am the Lord your G-d."

The Meaning
and Power of Silence

This *Parshah*, *Aharei Mot*, opens with a discussion of the laws of priestly purity, especially as they relate to the holiest day of the year—Yom Kippur—the Day of Atonement. These laws are preceded by reminding the priestly clan of the sudden deaths of Nadav and Avihu, the sons of Aaron the high priest, which was discussed earlier. Why is this reminder necessary now? To answer this question, one would be well advised to examine more closely Aaron's reaction upon hearing the tragic news, "Aaron was silent" (Lev. 10:3). Whereas some would consider his response as strange or inadequate, from a psychological perspective it is quite understandable. In the face of tragedy, words fail. Screams or sighs are involuntary attempts to surpass words, but silence is often the sole means of expressing the intensity of grief in the face of an unexpected loss.

Rabbi Joseph B. Soloveitchick, Z"L, in one of his public lectures discusses the human reaction to death as an outcry of horror and grief. Man responds to his defeat at the hands of death with feelings of self-devastation and utter despair. He states that in the first stage of mourning prior to burial, the *Halachah* wisely exempts the mourner from performing religious rituals such as attending daily services, because the shock inhibits speech. One can just imagine Aaron's feelings of total helplessness in confronting the awesome power of death. From a psychological perspective, Aaron's reaction of silence is a form of regression from human to primitive animal, where there is no speech but only instinctual pain that can be expressed by a howl, outcry and/or muted silence. In this stage of blackness and helplessness one is incapable of action. However, once the initial shock is over, then ritual comes into play as a bridge from helplessness to normal functioning. That explains the juxtaposition of remembering the tragic death of Aaron's two sons with all of his ritual responsibilities on Yom Kippur. Return to religious and social functioning is the beginning step in Aaron's healing process of mourning.

Of all the losses one experiences in life, the death of a child is perhaps the most devastating. This experience was demonstrated to me in the words of a woman patient, "There are no words deep enough to describe my pain. The only thing that feels right is the howl of pain like a wounded animal." Aaron's silence is an inaudible expression of this woman's deep sadness. It was, therefore, necessary to break this pattern of psychological solitude and silence by engaging Aaron once again into a carefully outlined regimen of Yom Kippur activities.

Aaron's reaction of silence also helps explain a traditional Jewish mourning practice. One is discouraged from visiting or comforting mourners prior to the burial. At this time of initial loss, silence and separation are necessary in order for mourners to express grief in private with members of their immediate family. After the burial, when the full reality of the inconsolable loss begins to set in, words of comfort can be heard, when the mourners are psychologically ready to receive comfort from others. The emotions of shock and disbelief obviously overcame Aaron at the moment of greatest joy in his investiture as the first high priest of Israel. On Yom Kippur, however, he is then in a psychological state when he can listen and understand the awesome responsibility that is his, as a counter balance to his prestigious position and status. G-d asks Moses to speak to Aaron and give him instructions on the activities necessary in conducting the Yom Kippur rituals. G-d is giving Moses a pattern of behavior to help Aaron overcome his silence, shock, helplessness and grief.

The first thing Aaron must do on Yom Kippur is to bring "a young bullock for a sin offering and a ram for a burnt-offering." Accordingly, Aaron's first act on Yom Kippur was to seek atonement for his own sins (Lev. 16:3). Why begin the holiest day of the year for the people by implying its holiest person is guilty of sin? Could this sin offering be linked to the death of Aaron's two sons, implying that Aaron felt some personal guilt over their deaths? If so, (a common reaction to sudden loss), G-d is giving Aaron a means to absolve this guilt by bringing a sin offering as stated, "And Aaron shall present the bullock of the sin offering, which is for himself, and shall make atonement for himself and for his house" (Lev. 16:11).

Before Aaron can seek forgiveness for the Children of Israel, he must first address his own failings vis-à-vis his role in the golden calf and all it represented. That is why the *Parshah* concludes with prohibitions against unchastity, unlawful marriages and Moloch worship which are all associated with idolatrous practices. Aaron is, therefore, reminded that the "strange fire" that caused his sons' demise may be related to his role in forging the golden calf. Now, however, is the time for Aaron to seek forgiveness by bringing a sin offering in order to proceed from grief to reparation, and to the great goal of strengthening the religious structure of the new nation.

Kedoshim
Leviticus 19:1-20:27
A Manual of Moral Instruction

*T*his Parshah, especially chapter 19, is generally considered the Torah's closest formulation of a Code of Holiness, as it states in its opening words, "Ye shall be holy, for I, the Lord your G-d am holy." It proceeds to state a whole series of "thou shalts": honoring parents and the elderly, observing the Sabbath, consideration of the poor; love your neighbor as yourself, concern for the stranger and the disabled, and many more "thou shalt nots": idolatry, theft, false oaths, gossip, perversion of justice, seeking revenge, bearing a grudge, cross-breeding, gluttony, witchcraft, tattooing, etc. The Israelites are again warned not to go in the abhorrent ways of the surrounding nations, lest they be exiled from the Promised Land. They must always remember that as a holy people they are set apart as G-d's Chosen ones and should act accordingly.

G-d: First Interpreter
of the Unconscious

This *Parshah*, *Kedoshim* (Holy), specifically chapter 19, represents G-d's call to Israel as the path to take in achieving holiness. Chapter 19, with its many ethical and ritual precepts, is considered the closest Torah formulation to a holiness code, as it also makes reference in its verses to the Decalogue, the Ten Commandments. What is not readily apparent, however, are the psychological issues embedded in the unconsciousness of man that precipitate the need for this moral code.

First, we need to broadly describe what is meant by the unconscious. The unconscious is that part of the psyche that holds the psychic material not in one's immediate field of awareness. Ideas, experiences, feelings, associations and impulses lie hidden in this unseen landscape of the unconscious. Evidence of the workings of the unconscious is most commonly seen in dreams, slips of the tongue, psychosomatic symptoms and reacting at times in ways we don't understand. It is the cauldron of these untamed feelings and impulses that are often hidden from the human consciousness. For example, in this Parshah, there is a listing of forbidden relationships, particularly incestuous ones.

How difficult it is for a person who is unfamiliar with his unconscious yearnings and impulses to recognize the oedipal feelings of the young child towards his parents. The child wishes to have the parent of the opposite sex to himself and has competitive feelings toward the same sex parent. Eventually, as the child matures, he learns to accept the same sex parent and recognizes that the opposite sex parent cannot be his alone. This natural incestuous wish becomes tamed by appropriate parental guidance and by the boundaries set by the Torah in this *Parshah*, which forbid incestuous relationships. It is also not unusual for a male parent to find himself having sexual feelings for his adolescent daughter. After all, the daughter is in many ways a reminder of his wife, to whom he was attracted in his youth. The Torah therefore states, "Profane not thy daughter otherwise she will become a harlot, lest the land fall into harlotry and lewdness" (Lev. 19:29).

Sisters and brothers may be tempted at times to act out sexual feelings because they are in such close intimate contact. The Torah in this Parshah implicitly recognizes these unconscious feelings and impulses, which are only forbidden when they are acted out. In other words, G-d understands these unconscious human yearnings as natural. Therefore, it is necessary for humans to learn to control them, which is the purpose for setting incestuous boundaries.

Similarly, establishing the laws of honesty in this *Parshah* is an implicit recognition of the unconscious human impulses of greed and jealousy. The Torah states, "Ye shall not steal, neither shall ye deal falsely, nor lie to one another. Thou shall not hate your brother in your heart, nor stand idly by the blood of thy neighbor… but thou shall love thy neighbor as thyself" (Lev. 19:11-18). In order to tame our greed, we are told to leave the corners of our fields for the poor. This is a tacit recognition that our internal unconscious forces may not be as generous in giving to others.

It has been my professional experience that when a patient reaches a level of maturity in his relationships to family and friends, the person begins to search for what is called "spirituality." In chapter 19, one is given a "how to" blueprint to achieve this goal. The holiness code in *Parshat Kedoshim* is the Torah's path to holiness and spirituality. It consists of a combination of ethical precepts between man and man, as well as spiritual or ritual practices in relating to G-d. Whereas these precepts are not in any particular order and are devoid of an overarching philosophy, they are profound in their simplicity, "Speak to the children of Israel and say unto them, 'Ye shall be holy, for I, the Lord your G-d am holy" (Lev. 19:2).

With the advent of elements of the Decalogue in this *Parshah*, G-d further emphasizes the role of the unconscious. The basic rationale runs as follows: there are natural psychological impulses that every human possesses. In order to effectively deal with these issues of sexuality, perversity, greed, envy and rage, we must make ourselves aware of what drives our psyche or *yetzer hara* (evil inclination). Our mission is to make these unconscious forces conscious. Then one can choose to take charge of these feelings. This differentiates us from animals, in that we can speak, think and choose, whereas animals are motivated solely by instincts. This mandate to be holy is man's directive to be separate and different from animals. Part of "raising the bar" for human beings is our ability to make the unconscious conscious, once we are guided to do so by way of the ethical precepts in chapter 19.

One of the most startling side effects I have witnessed in both psychoanalysis and psychotherapy is when there is growth in psychological maturity there is a concurrent emerging quest for spirituality. This may be due to diminishing narcissism and self-involvement which now leave an opening for another object—spirituality. There may also have been an experience of trust and care in therapy that sponsors this belief and hope that there is a higher force than oneself which can care for us. The issue is certainly not closed as to the cause, but the results of successful treatment have moved patients to a greater need for the "other" and greater trust in a Higher Being. The feeling of emptiness that many patients feel when entering in a therapeutic relationship find partial resolution through successful therapy. Somehow, however, the unconscious yearns for more. This unconscious need for spirituality is addressed in this simple, yet profound call, "Ye shall be holy, because I the Lord am holy."

Emor
Leviticus 21:1-24:23
Holiness of the Sanctuary

*I*n view of the special religious role played by the priests, the standards of ritual purity are higher for them than for others. This entails avoiding contact with the dead and attending funerals, except for their seven closest relatives. Priests with certain physical defects were not permitted to officiate in the Sanctuary. Likewise, animals used for sacrifice were required to be without any physical blemish. No animal could be sacrificed prior to eight days after birth. These and many other regulations concerning the offering of animal sacrifices are detailed under the general principles of hallowing G-d's name (Kiddush Hashem), a principle that applies to all Israel. The Parshah then presents a detailed description of the various holy days in the Jewish lunar calendar and the many observances associated with them. It begins with the weekly Sabbath and proceeds seriatim from the Festival of Passover which occurs at dusk on the 14th day of the first month, Nisan, followed by Shavuoth (Festival of Weeks), then Rosh Hashanah on the first day of the seventh month, Yom Kippur and closing with Sukkoth, Feast of Tabernacles. The Parshah concludes with specifying the daily task of the priest to see that the Menorah (lamp) burns continually in the Sanctuary, and also their obligations to tend to arranging of the shewbread.

Priesthood:
Privilege or Liability?

In many areas of religious life, whether one is a *Kohen* (priest), a Rabbi, community leader, or a person of great wealth and influence, the fantasy is that this privileged status gives one license, at times, to go beyond the boundaries of ethical behavior. In this *Parshah*, which discusses regulations concerning priests and the Sanctuary, we are reminded that a priest, who has privilege, is obligated to conduct himself with greater responsibility than *Amcha* (the rank and file). Because of their privileged position, the priests who are in the public eye, have an added responsibility to serve as examples for others. Moreover, certain restrictions are placed upon them as it is stated, "There shall none defile himself for the dead among his people, except for his kin, that is near unto him, for his mother and for his father, and for his son, and for his daughter... he shall not defile himself, being a chief man among his people, to profane himself" (Lev. 21:1-3). Whereas priests could not attend funerals except for their immediate families, this restriction was even more severe for the high priest, who is endowed with the highest level of sanctity, "neither shall he go into any dead body, nor defile himself [even] for his father and mother" (Lev. 21:11). Clearly this added restriction demonstrates that exalted status does not confer greater license or omnipotence, but greater responsibilities (*noblesse oblige*).

The priest has another restriction which has psychological ramifications. A priest who has a *mum* (physical disability) is disqualified from officiating in the Sanctuary. He can, however, maintain his priestly status, eat from the sacrifices and perform special responsibilities indirectly related to the service. The sacrifices offered in the Sanctuary, however, required a higher level of perfection, whether it is the priestly officiant or the animal that is being sacrificed. A priest who suffers from certain physical defects is, therefore, exempt from serving in the Sanctuary. To some, this may sound discriminatory, but the Torah is actually exhibiting great psychological insight in this issue. It is quite natural for a person with a physical disability to feel psychologically deficient. This narcissistic injury to one's psyche can sometimes motivate a person to seek special favors to compensate for the loss in order to prove one's self-worth. This would render this person too vulnerable to uphold the high standards of leadership, and liable to misuse his position as a means to restitute the psychological wound. Apparently the Torah sensed these emotional difficulties in setting up stringent rules governing the activities of the priests who were leading the services in the Sanctuary.

When it comes to leadership, because the burdens are heavy and the demands are intense, not everyone is psychologically equipped to handle these demands. They may find themselves lacking the courage, stamina and moral strength to cope with the demands of leadership. The priests, on the one hand, are community figures enjoying public recognition by virtue of their status, but who on the other hand are gauged by a higher standard that involves increased responsibilities and restrictions.

In the high standards of maintaining ritual purity and of the general behavior expected of priests, one can inferentially see a benefit for the people. These standards and rules protect the people from the abuse of power by a wayward priest. We are painfully aware of sexual abuse by clergy and teachers, which has recently come to light. The most egregious is the sexual abuse of children and the belated psychological toll this abuse inflicts upon the victims. Unfortunately, this abuse of power is played out on many levels of society. We see it also in patient-therapist relationships, where there have been cases of therapists taking advantage of their position of power to verbally/ sexually abuse the vulnerable patient. To prevent this from happening, the aspiring psychoanalyst must go through personal psychoanalysis to prevent acting out on the patient one's own personal issues. This *Parshah* provides a strict venue to prevent the abuse of priestly power. Great care and skill must be exercised by the priests in following the exacting protocol. Any abuse of the system invalidates their right to perform the rituals especially in the main Sanctuary. Privilege carries with it liability. Those in power positions are well advised to maintain a proper balance between them.

Behar
Leviticus 25:1-26:2
The Sabbatical and Jubilee Years

In this Parshah we are introduced to the concept of a Sabbatical year —Shemitah, when the land rests after six years of productivity. This is followed by a Jubilee year—Yovel—on the fiftieth year after seven consecutive Sabbatical years. The Jubilee year is proclaimed on Yom Kippur with the sounding of the shofar (ram's horn), which signals the release of all Hebrew servants, and return of property to its original owner, except for house property in a walled city. God promises that sufficient crops will grow during the years of productivity to off set leaving the fields fallow during the Sabbatical years. Various regulations are given governing the redemption of land and houses during the Jubilee year. Certain rights are given the Israelite servant to prevent permanent servitude.

Is it Better to Lease or to Own?

In this *Parshah*, *Behar*, G-d expands the purview of Sabbath observance to include land as well as humans and animals. "In the Sabbatical [seventh] year, the land is to rest [lie fallow], it is a Sabbath unto the Lord; thou shalt not reap, thou shalt not gather" (Lev. 25:4). At the conclusion of seven Sabbatical years, "Ye shall hallow the fiftieth year and proclaim liberty throughout the land unto all the inhabitants thereof; it shall be a Jubilee unto you; And ye shall return every man unto his [original] possession, and ye shall return every man unto his family" (Lev. 25:10). The *Parshah* concludes with reiteration of the second commandment against worshiping idols/other gods.

These opening and closing themes encapsulate a fundamental way of viewing possessions which have psychological as well as theological implications. To illustrate this point in modern terms; let us say that a person is interested in acquiring a new car. Should he buy or lease? There are pros and cons concerning which option to take. In the case of a lease, at the conclusion of the lease period, the car is returned to the dealership, whereas in sales, the car remains with the buyer. In Biblical terms, however, even the purchaser of land must return it in the Jubilee year to its original owner, in effect acknowledging that the land was actually leased. Similarly with the Hebrew bondsman who was sold into slavery was actually leased, because in the fiftieth year he was freed.

On a grander scale, the Torah is teaching us that all "possessions," whether land, humans or wealth are on loan for a certain length of time, but everything ultimately returns to the Creator. That is why the *Parshah* concludes with the second commandment admonishing mankind not to worship other gods, or graven images, that is, mate- rial objects such as land, money or physical possessions which are transient. Idealization of money, property and/or power is a form of idol worship and an illusion. In the end, humans die. Possessions are not permanent and power comes and goes. Eventually one comes to the conclusion as did the wise King Solomon in his latter years, *ha-kol hevel,* "all is vanity" (Eccl. 1:2). Everything is on lease for a longer or shorter period until the Jubilee year when it returns to its original owner, G-d.

It is not unusual for me to hear certain patients state, "If only I had that piece of art work, or if only I could be the C.E.O. of the company, I would be alright, I would be a somebody." They feel that material wealth or power would give them a sense of mastery and control over others, and that self-esteem can be purchased with the next major acquisition. This may lead to a "momentary high", only for it to come crashing down afterwards with a greater sense of emptiness and despair. Unfortunately, the search for well-being through owning possessions turns out to be an unending frustrating endeavor.

Psychological research demonstrates that material wealth does not correlate well with life satisfaction or happiness. In fact, the drive of acquisitiveness often leads to depression and neuroticism. Who can forget the Oscar winning film *Citizen Kane*, starring Orson Welles, which has served as a long-standing example of the materialistic quest which left the collector at the end of his life, a lonely disillusioned man bereft of family and friends. Sheldon and Kasser, in their research on this subject, found that psychological well-being is optimized when the different and/or conflicting aspects of personality are integrated into a harmonious whole. What this means is that a person with a religious value system may have components of acquisitiveness or self-centeredness as long as they are balanced and integrated into one's personality. It does not have to be "either/or."

The lesson of the Jubilee year is a painful lesson the Israelites experienced beginning with the exodus when they turned to the worship of golden images in their mistaken belief that they could forge a god to lead them. At various times in Jewish history, after attaining material possessions they were expelled from Spain, England, France and Germany. The portable Torah and its teachings, however, accompanied them wherever they went. While addressed to the generations of freed Egyptian slaves, the Sabbatical/Jubilee years coupled with the admonition against worshiping other gods resonates even today with current generations. They not only present a polemic against the false gods of ownership, but provide a deeper insight into the human psyche. They remind us of who is the true Owner and Creator of the universe and who is in ultimate control. They remind us of the important role of the spiritual in human affairs. One's mission on this earth, whether longer or shorter, is not to exploit fellow humans, but to enjoy G-d's blessings provided for us by conducting oneself in accordance with the ethical principles laid out in the Torah.

Behukotai
Leviticus 26:3-27:34
Warnings against Disobedience

*T*he concluding Parshah in the Book of Leviticus sums up the blessings the Israelites will enjoy if they observe G-d's law, but more so, the evil that will befall them if they choose to disobey the Torah. Repentance is the route to gain restoration. Returning to the theme of upkeep of the Sanctuary which opened the Book of Leviticus, this Parshah delineates ways in which a person can assess the means to help sustain the service of the Sanctuary.

The Proverbial "If"

As we come to the end of the book of Leviticus, it is time for Moses to recapitulate the importance of adhering to the new law, lest the recently freed slaves lapse into the perversity of Egypt. This *Parshah, Behukotai* (My Laws) opens with the prophetic forecast, "If ye walk in My statutes, and keep My commandments and do them… you will enjoy the blessings of plenty and peace…. But if ye will not hearken unto Me and you will not do all these commandments …you will suffer destruction and exile" (Lev. 26:3-39).

The key word in determining the fate of Israel regarding reward or punishment is the proverbial *im*, "If." As a free and independent people your destiny is no longer determined by Egypt, but by your own free choice. This fateful choice confronting the Israelites is comparable to the family setting when the child reaches the point of maturity and is ready to make informed intelligent decisions in life. The Israelites in the desert are still in their infancy as a nation, enjoying the guidance of an unseen G-d, represented by, "a cloud by day and a pillar of fire by night" and a nurturing parental figure in the person of Moses. In this infantile state, the Torah spells out in horrific terms *tochachah* (admonition) the full extent of punishment that will befall the Children of Israel "if "they choose to be disobedient.

This is the equivalent of parents trying to teach their young children how to behave, by pointing out what will happen if they misbehave, "If you touch a hot stove, you will burn your hand." In the case of the Children of Israel, their attraction to idols destroys the very essence of who they are as a distinct people. This is the psychological price they will have to pay for their betrayal, a loss of identity. The *tochachah* is the Torah's gruesome description of the external physical punishment, but the internal psychological damage is even greater. They will lose their unique identity as G-d's chosen people by defying His will and following in the immoral ways of the idolatrous. They are now blessed with free choice "if" they choose wisely between these two very distinct opposites.

With the admonition of the consequences the Israelites face by their free choice, we come to the end of the book of Leviticus. The "ball is in their court," as they can no longer blame the Egyptians for their suffering. In this book of Leviticus, they are given a "shorthand" blueprint of the "good life" as spelled out in *Parshat Kedoshim*. Whereas, this third book of the Torah dwells largely on matters relating to the priests and the Sanctuary, the underlying message is addressed to all Israel. The priests, as the religious leaders, must assume the awesome responsibilities of their exalted office. The consequences of violation of this trust resulted in the tragic death of Aaron's two sons. Are the Israelites mature enough to accept the responsibilities of freedom and make the appropriate free choices reflecting growing independence, or are they still psychologically tied to the Egyptian slave mentality of dependency and stagnation? At this point, with the basic principles of the civil and religious law in place, the Israelites will again be put to the test in the events that follow in the next book, Numbers.

THE BOOK OF NUMBERS

"And the Lord spoke unto Moses in the Wilderness of Sinai...
'Take ye the sum of all the congregation of the children of Israel'"
— *Numbers 1:1-2*

Bamidbar
Numbers 1:1-4:20
Numbering of the Israelites

*T*he Book of Numbers opens with G-d speaking to Moses on the first day of the second month in the second year since their exodus from Egypt. His instructions are to take a census of all men of military age from age twenty and up. There follows a breakdown by tribes, which total 603,550 soldiers. The tribe of Judah numbering 74,600 is the largest of all the tribes. The tribes are then arranged in certain positions around the Mishkan (Tent of Meeting), which positions are kept in their marching orders through the wilderness. The Levites who are in charge of the Tent of Meeting in the center of the camp are instructed as to their special duties. A census is taken of the Levites, who are exempt from military service because of their responsibilities in the upkeep of the Mishkan. Unlike the other tribes, their service begins at age thirty up to age fifty. Their duties vary according to the heads of their families. The specific duties assigned to the extended family of Kohath the son of Levi, concludes this week's Torah reading.

The Inception of Urban Planning in the Wilderness of Sinai

The opening chapter in the Book of Numbers, Bamidbar, finds the Israelites ensconced in the wilderness of Sinai. It is at this juncture that the Torah steps back and takes stock of the numbers within the various tribes. In so doing, it records that the Israelites were able to maintain their numbers since leaving Egypt in spite of all of the challenges presented by an arid wilderness. An important factor accounting for this is what may be termed today as "urban planning." The first consideration in urban planning is safety/security. This is reflected in the census taken of the number of males in each tribe age twenty and over who serve in the army which total over 600,000 soldiers. Whereas they are attached to their respective tribes, certain tribes are designated to march together, giving them greater security and a greater feeling of togetherness. In order to further this feeling of unity, all twelve tribes are divided into units of three situated around the four directions of the central Tent of Meeting i.e. the Mishkan.

The tribe of Levi does not serve in the army because it ministers to the physical needs of the *Mishkan* and to its sacrificial rituals via its subsidiary priestly clan headed by Aaron. The Levites serve as the inner guard situated around the central *Mishkan*. This sophisticated demographic plan helps provide order for a mobile population estimated at over three million souls, facilitating its development under the most trying circumstances of living in the wilderness. Despite the lack of hospitals, doctors, and modern medicine, their very survival is a commentary on this demographic plan to create separate tribes, with built-in safeguards designed to provide a protected and productive environment.

The overriding spiritual consideration underlying this advanced societal design is *Kedushah*. As discussed earlier, this is the importance of molding this fledgling nation into a separate special people dedicated to G-d according to the dictates of the Torah. This planned community, therefore, was designed to keep out other foreign idolatrous and unethical influences. What better place to cultivate this goal than in the wilderness, away from Egypt and other idolatrous nations.

Urban planning, as seen in this *Parshah*, is structured around physical and spiritual safeguards. The patriarchal structure built around heads of families served as the basic social infrastructure. This facilitated inter-communication at a time when the means of mass communication was unknown. The *Mishkan*, located in the center of the camp, served both demographically and spiritually as the central rallying point for all important events. These safeguards, together with the standing army, served as the secure framework that was conducive for physical growth. These were the externals. Internal spiritual growth was provided by the boundaries and values set forth in the Torah. These safeguards and boundaries together helped constitute this early example of "urban planning" that may explain how such a large mobile population could survive and even grow in what appears to be forty years of aimless wandering in the desert.

A psychological parallel of this concern for safeguards is evident in the physical design of the therapeutic relationship. In terms of safety and confidentiality, the consulting room must be soundproof. There is to be a safe distance between the patient and therapist. It is also understood that "everything is grist for the mill" of dialogue without fear of verbal retaliation or emotional harm caused by the therapist. This is basically the foundation for building trust and safety which allows the patient to move forward from the place where he/she is stuck to a higher level of maturity.

Another aspect of the therapeutic relationship besides issues of safety and trust is the patient's inability to establish personalized connections and relationships. This is due, in part, to the impersonal technological era in which we live today which fosters anonymity. This is especially true for those living in high rise buildings and overpopulated areas. This demographic reality exacerbates the socializing difficulties of those patients who already feel isolated and alienated. It is one of the built-in advantages of those who feel strongly connected by religion and culture, that they are encouraged to reach out to their neighbors and develop closer relationships despite urban sprawl. It is this concern about "urban planning" being developed by the Israelites in the wilderness that assigns physical "space" between the tribes to maintain individuality, yet share responsibilities for further collaboration and sociability. In this sense, what we see unfolding in this opening *Parshah* in the Book of Numbers, is a demographic urban plan that is instructive to us both in its external physical design as well as to furthering its spiritual and ethical goals. This combined plan not only accounts for their physical survival in the wilderness, but perpetuates their developmental growth as a maturing people under the most adverse of environmental conditions.

Naso
Numbers 4:21-7:89
Levitical Census

*T*his Parshah continues the census of the tribe of Levi with a description of its respective duties, specifically of the extended families of Gershon and Merari, sons of Levi. The census reveals a total of 8,580 males between the ages of thirty to fifty who are eligible to serve in the Mishkan.

The Torah describes in detail the ordeal of jealousy when a husband suspects his wife of infidelity. She is known in Hebrew as a Sotah. The drinking of the "water of bitterness" and the accompanying oath are imposed only as a last resort, if she refuses to confess. If, indeed, she is innocent, the waters have no effect and she will be able to conceive, otherwise the waters will cause premature death. This is followed by the law of the Nazirite, one who vows to undertake a program of austerity designed to induce greater spirituality and purity. The vow of the Nazirite was time bound, after which period he could take a haircut, drink intoxicants and return to normal life. He or she would, however, be required to bring a sin offering as part of the rite to be performed at the completion of the vow. Aaron and his sons are then instructed the Hebrew formula for the threefold priestly blessing of the Children of Israel. The Parshah concludes with a description of the identical gifts brought by the princes of each of the twelve tribes over a period of twelve days after the dedication of the Mishkan.

Repetition,
Restitution and Restoration

Patients will often come to me to discuss a so-called "crisis." This usually means that someone has wronged, ignored or hurt them in some real or imagined way. In the search for the true meaning of this crisis, I find that this "crisis" has recurred in the person's life, although frequently masked and disguised. It may have the outward appearance of a new and different situation, but more often it is a disguised version of an unresolved developmental issue. This often leaves the patient "arrested" at a lower developmental level, preventing movement forward in one's psychological growth. The patient is unaware that these "crises" are really attempts to conquer a long-standing personal issue. Since the patient repeats the same method of resolution, the solution usually fails. For example, a woman marries an alcoholic which causes a crisis leading to divorce, and she swears never to marry another alcoholic. Lo and behold, she remarries a man who looks different, acts and talks differently, but turns out to be another alcoholic. There is some unconscious need in this woman to repeat her masochistic role in the marriage. This is not unlike the saying, "I have met the enemy and behold it is I." Unless the patient is willing to see this unconscious motivation, the so-called crisis continues throughout life. Once her role in creating the crisis is understood, she can then begin to extricate herself from these repetitious acts.

The psychological dynamics discussed above are present in the behavior of a perpetrator who wrongs another as noted in this week's Torah portion, *Naso*. "When a man or woman shall commit any sin that men commit, to commit a trespass against

173

the Lord and that soul be guilty; then they shall confess their sin which they have done; and he shall make restitution for his guilt in full, and add unto it the fifth part thereof, and give it unto him in respect of whom he hath been guilty" (Num. 5:6-7). On the surface, this restitution, plus the fine, is punishment for aggressive behavior against another, e.g., theft, cheating, etc.; the fine should serve as a deterrent to future repetition. The Torah is hinting that aggressive behavior against another carries with it an internal flaw in the perpetrator. Restitution to the victim must, therefore, be accompanied with a confession which begins the process of introspection, to look internally to find the cause of the aggression. This aggression is not only against the other person, but on a deeper psychological level an admission, albeit unconscious, of a masochistic need to punish oneself. The confession is necessary so that the aggressor will begin to recognize that restitution is not only an external punishment, but an internal process of overcoming these feelings as well.

These same psychological dynamics are found in the ordeal of the Sotah, the married woman suspected by her husband of infidelity which is discussed in this Parshah. The Torah describes in vivid detail the rite the Sotah is subjected to, in drinking the bitter waters and then observing the aftermath, in order to ascertain her guilt or innocence (Num. 5:11-31). Without commenting on the feminist movement's revulsion against this ancient and demeaning ritual, in terms of its psychological aspects we see again the Torah's emphasis upon confession as a means of removing guilt. Administering the bitter waters is only imposed as a last resort, if the suspected wife does not confess. What is sought more than physical punishment is her voluntary confession to counteract her husband's feelings of guilt and jealousy. Guilt is not only the burden of the suspected wife, but also of the husband in not having been attentive to the emotional needs of his wife. Unbridled jealousy on the part of an authoritative husband, who is threatened if his wife is not totally submissive, could be an underlying issue in their deteriorating relationship. Restitution is, therefore, not only a physical act of repayment for an offense, but a means of restoring self esteem to both injured parties, the aggressor and the victim.

In the case of the *Sotah* who may have strayed, she may be trying inappropriately to restitute her self esteem by saying to herself, "someone else loves me." This false restitution not only indicates a moral flaw, but a psychological delusion that someone else can make her whole. This lack of self-awareness guarantees that the act will be repeated, similar to the case of the distraught woman who remarries an alcoholic. The *Sotah*'s partner, the aggressor, suffers a similar fate in feeling hurt and jealous over her rejection of him. The tenth commandment, not to lust after your neighbor's wife, is also not just a moral issue, but may be a symptom of an underlying psychological deficit "in the eyes of the beholder" which needs to be addressed. Drinking of the bitter waters by the suspected *Sotah*, although targeting only the woman, is an attempt to have a ritual which will repair the guilt and anger experienced on both sides. Both parties have to walk away from the test feeling psychologically restored in order to resume their relationship.

In this case of the *Sotah* as well as in the previous one, the object is not so much on the consequences of sin, that is, on the punitive measures taken against the alleged off ender. It is rather on the process of examining the internal cause(s) of the sin, whether ritually against G-d or acted out on one's spouse. The process begins with a verbal confession that is the equivalent to the patient's narrative in therapy. Behavior change begins with becoming aware and examining one's *modus operandi*. It is through the patient's verbal narratives that the therapist gains an insight into the person's psyche. This is the avenue one should take to cope with emotions of guilt and jealousy leading toward the prospect of restoration of a healthy psyche.

The Torah, in discussing these rituals, is delving into the intricate internal process needed to restore the individual to spiritual health. The ordeal of the Sotah is a commentary on the primitive realities of spousal relationships that existed in Biblical times. Nevertheless, the underlying psychological issues of jealousy and trust in marital relationships still remain a leading cause for couples seeking treatment in our times.

Beha'alotcha
Numbers 8:1-12:16
Murmurings and Rebellions

*A*aron is instructed the procedures to be followed when lighting the lamps in the seven-branched Menorah, candelabrum. The Levites are officially dedicated into their service in the Mishkan in a special ceremony. A second Passover is permitted one month later for those who, due to issues of impurity and excessive travel, were unable to participate in the paschal offering on the fourteenth of Nisan. The Israelites are reminded that the fiery cloud over the Mishkan serves as G-d's beacon to guide them on their travels in the wilderness. Two silver clarions are to be used to summon the Israelites for announcements, and when to march in special tribal formations.

Moses invites his father-in-law, Jethro, to remain with them, but he decides to return to his native Midian. As the camp is ready to continue their journey, Moses recites a special prayer imploring G-d's presence and protection in their travels. At the instigation of those non-Hebrews who joined the Israelites in their exodus from Egypt, a series of rebellions erupt. They complain about their daily diet of Manna and the absence of meat. Moses, in turn, complains about the weight of his responsibilities, to which G-d responds by instructing him to appoint seventy elders to assist him. As to the people's dietary complaint, G-d sends an abundance of quail which they devour ravenously until they are sickened by it, as G-d predicted. A plague breaks out as punishment for their rebelliousness. Even Miriam and Aaron are not immune from maligning their brother, Moses, which results in Miriam being afflicted with a serious skin disease. Moses prays for her recovery, and she is restored to health enabling the people to resume their journey.

Status Issues: Who is on Top?

The Torah portrays Moses as this towering spiritual figure who, as liberator and lawgiver, dominates four books of the Pentateuch yet we are given precious few glimpses into his personal family life. In this week's Torah portion, *Beha'alotcha*, we are given two instances of family involvement. The first example of family involvement is indirect by way of a metaphor. Moses is so exasperated by the people's constant complaints, this time over the lack of meat, that he bemoans his fate as follows, "Have I conceived all this people, have I given birth to them that Thou shouldst say unto me, 'Carry them in thy bosom as a nurse carries the suckling children...'" (Num. 11:12).

This metaphor is a psychological allusion to his own troubled birth and being an adopted child of the Egyptian princess. Now he is expected to be the nurturing parental figure to this unruly adopted child—Israel. We have seen in previous *Parshiyot* that indeed, the people viewed Moses as a kind of father figure. Here, however, Moses tenders his resignation from this unwanted "transference" parental role, "I am not able to bear this people alone, because it is too heavy for me. And if Thou deals thus with me, kill me, I pray Thee..." (Num. 11:15). At this point, G-d relieves Moses of his angst by advising him to appoint seventy elders to assist him.

The second instance of a more personal family nature, is an episode of envy and recrimination by Miriam and Aaron against their youngest brother, which is reminiscent of the sibling rivalry experienced in the patriarchal families. "And Miriam and Aaron spoke against Moses because of the Cushite woman he had married... And they said, 'Hath the Lord indeed only spoken with Moses? Hath He not spoken also with us?'"(Num. 12:1-3). The Midrash targets Miriam as the main instigator, as she is later punished with a serious skin disease, an affliction associated with *lashon hara* (evil talk).

Why is it necessary for the Torah to even record this personal family squabble, which comes as a kind of postscript in a *Parshah* dealing with important communal matters, such as the induction of the seventy elders, observing the second Passover, dedication of Levites, etc.? The Torah is apparently showing the destructiveness of Miriam's envy of Moses which is projected onto the Cushite woman. Favoritism, real or imagined, invariably engenders feelings of jealousy in being overlooked or displaced. Miriam and Aaron, in spite of their acknowledged leadership and status, are not immune from these emotions.

In a recent article in the *Chicago Tribune* it was reported that first-born children are often the best C.E.O.s. Their early experience of "bossing around" their younger siblings seems to hone their leadership skills. This *Parshah* demonstrates an interesting outcome when the process is reversed. What is the state of the family structure when the youngest child surpasses the older siblings? Moses was taken from his home at infancy, and raised in the royal palace by the Egyptian princess, with his mother, Yocheved, serving as his wet nurse. We can assume that while her mother was absent, Miriam, the older sister, had additional household responsibilities. Meanwhile Moses enjoys the position of being the special child to the princess and to his mother. In his adult years he is again chosen to be special, this time to become the servant of G-d to lead his people to freedom. Miriam and Aaron, as evidenced by the above text, are harboring feelings of jealousy at the disruption of the traditional family power structure. Miriam proceeds to displace her anger at Moses by maligning his Cushite wife. Unable to change the situation, she develops symptoms of a skin affliction called *tzaraat* in Hebrew, popularly translated as "leprosy." This physical reaction is also likely caused by her troubled emotional and psychological state.

It is well known that psychosomatic illness is an internalization of external problems that one cannot manage, that gets translated by the body into a language of physical symptoms. Miriam could not get the status she felt she deserved, so unconsciously she takes the anger out on herself. Attention is now focused on her body in the form of a skin malady. This is a distorted solution to her anger with Moses for usurping her position in the family and for turning the power in the family structure "upside-down." As partial punishment she is sent into isolation outside of the camp for seven days. The similarity of this period of time to the *Shivah* mourning period is no accident. The Torah is demonstrating an unconscious understanding that Miriam would need to go through a mourning period, by being separated from the community, in the same way as a mourner spends the *Shivah* period at home away from the rest of the community.

This period gives her the "space" to calm her anger and to mourn her real and perceived losses. Moses, displaying marked self-control over this sensitive family issue, invokes a very short but compelling prayer on behalf of Miriam's recovery, "And Moses cried out to the Lord saying: Heal her now, O G-d, I beseech Thee" (Num. 12:13). She is immediately cured, attesting to the efficacy and power of prayer in curing psychosomatic as well as physical illnesses. The *Parshah* concludes, "And the people journeyed not 'til Miriam was brought in [to the camp]" (Num. 12:15). This statement is a terse revealing commentary on the true standing and status that Miriam enjoyed with the people. It is also a sad commentary on how deep personal emotional issues, whether real or imagined, can get translated by the body into physical ailments. In this Miriam *lashon hara* episode, we see portrayed another example of the mind-body connection, in which the Midrash and modern psychology share similar insights.

Shelach
Numbers 13:1-15:41
The Spies' Demoralizing Report

*M*oses *dispatches twelve leaders representing each tribe to tour Canaan. They return after forty days with large clusters of grapes and with a discouraging report about the formidable enemy. The people lose faith in reaching the Promised Land and demand to return to Egypt. Caleb and Joshua, the only two scouts favoring the conquest, are threatened with their lives. G-d is enraged and condemns the people to languish in the wilderness for forty years corresponding to the forty days spent by the spies in Canaan. During this period, the generation that accepted the false report will die off, enabling the new generation raised in the wilderness to attain their objective. In desperation and in defiance of Moses, a premature attempt is made to enter Canaan and it is soundly defeated. The Parshah concludes with further instructions of certain priestly and ritual laws to be observed after the conquest. These include giving a portion of dough mixture, Hallah, to the priests, and the Mitzvah of Tzitzit, of placing fringes on four-cornered garments.*

Twelve Spies:
Two Character Models

In this week's Torah portion, Shelach, the evil report returned by ten of the twelve spies, contains an unusual metaphor that lends itself to psychological interpretation. Whereas, their initial report about the Promised Land and its inhabitants is descriptive and objective, "It is a land flowing with milk and honey. However, the people who dwell therein are powerful and the cities are fortified" (Num. 13:27-28), yet their conclusion is entirely subjective, "We were in our sight as grasshoppers, and so were we in their sight" (Num. 13:33). One can readily understand that compared to the children of Anak, who were reported to be giants, the spies must have appeared to them in poetic terms as tiny insects. Why would they, however, refer to themselves in such diminutive, derogatory terms when, in fact, these were the heads of the tribes?

Here is another example where psychological findings can prove to be instructive. Just as in dreams where the unconscious veils their meaning in often bizarre symbols, similarly here, the metaphor about insects veils the true inner cause behind their evil report. The admission by the ten spies that "we were in our sight as grasshoppers," betrays a basic characterological flaw in the psychological makeup of these so-called leaders. The report they brought back had more to say about their internal psychological landscape than with the external landscape they were ordered to survey. Their distorted vision that everyone else was bigger than life and more powerful, is really a reflection of how they viewed themselves as small, helpless creatures. This internal landscape caused a distorted vision of the land when projected out through the filter of their own insecurity and inferiority, "It is a land that devours its inhabitants and all the people are men of great stature" (Num. 13:32).

Caleb and Joshua, on the other hand, reported on the identical landscape and concluded, "Let us go up at once and possess it for we are well able to overcome it" (Num. 13:30). Their vision of the land derived from their own sense of themselves as strong, mature individuals. The filter that colored their view of the land derived not only from deep faith in G-d's mission, but from a sense of maturity, basic self-esteem and capacity to see themselves as equal to others. Fortified by these internal characteristics they reported, *tovah ha-aretz me'od me'od*, "The land is exceedingly good" (Num. 14:7).

Furthermore, they retain their positive sense of self and strength of character in the face of the dominant negative opinions of their peers and the masses. The internal character traits exhibited by Caleb and Joshua are recognized by G-d as the necessary qualifications for leadership in carrying out His will. These traits are in stark contrast to the insecure view of the ten, who when faced with possible adversity, regress to their slave mentality and to their infantile state of "running back to mommy," i.e., Egypt.

G-d, angered by their lack of faith, realizes that these "princes" lack the mature character requisites needed for leadership in carrying out His will. They are summarily dispatched like the insects they thought they were, along with the adult Egyptian-born generation that instigated this latest rebellion. G-d now symbolically reveals His desired character model by changing Joshua's Hebrew name from *Hoshea* to *Yehoshua*. Adding the prefix *yud* (first letter in G-d's name, YHWH) is indicative of G-d's spiritual bonding with Joshua. This means that Joshua, unlike the ten spies, possesses the mature leadership and character traits that warrant his becoming G-d's partner to succeed Moses. With the rise of a new, free generation raised in the wilderness, unfettered by the psychologically debilitating dependency of Egyptian bondage, the people are being psychologically conditioned to overcome adversity in order to enter the Promised Land.

There is currently a program for adolescents called the Wilderness Program, which is modeled after the experience of the Hebrews in the wilderness. The goal of this program is to develop maturity and self-esteem among troubled youth by having them learn to overcome the difficult forces of nature. We see how G-d's wilderness strategy of building psychological attributes of self-esteem and maturity among the Israelites is being implemented today with some of the same positive results. Jewish history continually reenacts this internal character struggle of autonomy vs. dependency, of maturity vs. immaturity, and the world views that flow from these models. The same method of conquering the external wilderness applies to coping with the internal struggles of the individual as well. Freud describes this psychological process using technical terminology discussed above, "Where the id was there ego shall be." This statement implies that the id, the internal wilderness of impulses within the human psyche, is conquered by making the unconscious conscious, by developing the ego (sense of self) in order to conquer the internal wilderness of the unknown.

The survival of Israel throughout the millennia is due, in no small measure, to the fact that it has succeeded in adopting the minority Joshua-Caleb character model in withstanding discrimination fostered by majority world opinion. It is this courageous minority report that enables the free wilderness generations to turn the tide against the Egyptian-born nay-sayers.

Korach
Numbers 16:1-18:32
The Korach Rebellion

*K*orach, a cousin of Moses, leads a rebellion against him supported by 250 community leaders as well as by Dathan and Abiram of the tribe of Reuven. They demand greater power sharing and accuse Moses and Aaron of self-interest. Moses proposes certain ritual trials consisting of incense censers, fire pans and rods in order to ascertain G-d's will. The ordeal ends with the rebel camp being engulfed in fire and buried in an earthquake. The fire-pans are preserved to cover the altar as a reminder of the authenticity of Moses and Aaron's leadership. The Parshah concludes with further enumeration of Levitical duties and with special gifts to be given to the priests.

Rebellion versus Creativity

Rebellion is a reaction against someone else's authority. In rebelling, the focus of the action is usually against someone else's leadership rather than for one's own positive agenda. If the rebellion succeeds, what often happens is the imposition of another form of oppressive authority to displace the former one, e.g., the French and Bolshevik revolutions. Aside from the political aspects of rebellion is the underlying psychological factor of envy, wanting to have the power enjoyed by the previous leader. This envy is usually a sign of some internal feeling of deficit which can only be redressed by forcibly wresting power from the other and by making it one's own. That is why rebellion is often accompanied with violence which invites a counter violent reaction. The alternative to rebellion is a peaceful autonomous act of creativity, to replace the unwanted authority with a workable substitute. Creativity is usually the result of "thinking out of the box" to form a new unthought-of solution. This creative stance implies an intuitive psychological awareness of one's own power and ability to find solutions without the necessity of taking it away from someone else.

The above dynamics of rebellion vs. creativity are dramatized in the unsuccessful rebellion led by Korach against his cousin Moses that we read about in this week's Torah reading. Moreover, this failed rebellion is a replay of the underlying psychological deficits of the ten spies which was discussed in the previous *Parshah*. These ten heads of their respective tribes regarded themselves as "insects," powerless and dependent, without any positive creative solutions

185

for overcoming the enemy. Joshua and Caleb, on the other hand, could see the world through their own sense of power and could, therefore, find creative solutions for entering the Promised Land. Korach, Dathan and Abiram, leaders of the rebellion, driven by their personal envy of Moses' authority, viewed the exercise of power as their sole agenda rather than offering a positive creative program for the welfare of the people. Since most of the rebels are Levites, who already enjoy higher status and power than their peers, Moses realizes what is their hidden agenda: "And ye will seek the priesthood also?" (Num. 16:10). He also senses in them the same self-serving defeatist character deficits that he associates with the ten spies. These spies are not worthy to lead as they would deter the people from achieving their goal of conquering Canaan.

In effect, these rebels are following in the spies' example with the same inevitable demoralizing result. "And it came to pass, as he made an end of speaking all these words that the ground did cleave asunder that was under them, and the earth opened her mouth and swallowed them up" (Num. 16:31-32).

The inherent issue of developmental stages in this *Parshah* is an important aspect of the story. The Israelites have struggled with many physical and psychological issues. They have been given the leadership of Moses as the father figure/emissary of G-d, and the Torah as a blueprint for establishing a safe and productive people both individually and as a group. The people begin to develop individually and collectively. They build the *Mishkan* using their individual talents and skills, and learn to work collaboratively. The people are given a test of psychological readiness when the spies are sent to view the land. The mixed results were: two spies (Joshua and Caleb) who saw the world through the window of their interior life as "can do"; and the ten spies who saw the world through their interior eyes as "can't do." Joshua and Caleb are ready to establish a collaborative community and to do the "heavy lifting" needed to establish themselves as an independent people with a land of their own. They have reached the developmental stage in peoplehood known psychologically as the second individuation or the equivalent of the stormy period of adolescence, marked by the struggle of psychological separation from parental authority figures. If successfully completed, the adolescent will be able to consolidate his identity as a male/female who has enough skills to accept responsibility and begin to think creatively of forging a career and family. The successful resolution of this period ends the need for rebellion against authority figures.

At this point in their travels and internal development, we are given here an example of an unsuccessfully accomplished adolescence. Korach apparently did not experience a stable family life. He felt he had not been treated fairly by his extended family as leadership was given to his cousins Moses and Aaron. His deprivation was manifest by his rebellion against authority figures in general and transferred to his cousin Moses. This common pre-oedipal drive to feel powerful only by destroying the power of the authority/father figure is aptly demonstrated by Korach. Instead of being able to fulfill his missing internal power by working creatively to establish himself as a powerful adult who is productive, he fantasizes that the destruction of the authority figure will cure his feeling of inferiority and inadequacy by diminishing the power of the other. This power will, in fantasy, be transferred from the authority figure to the aggressor (i.e. himself). This is a false substitute for the work needed to become mature and use one's own power creatively. Korach remains the eternal rebellious adolescent, angry at failing the second individuation. He is destroyed by his own internal rage as much as by the pit that engulfs him and his followers.

This episode is also a metaphor for the destructive power of envy which affects not only the "have nots," but the privileged as well. G-d is delivering a powerful psychological message to the Israelites about the dynamics of envy vs. creativity, about the importance of self-esteem vs. defeatism, and about what constitutes leadership. In the process, they witness another example of G-d intervening on behalf of Moses, who embodies those psychological virtues necessary for true leadership.

Hukkat
Numbers 19:1-22:1
The Mystery of the Red Heifer

*T*his Parshah opens with a mysterious rite involving a pure unyoked red heifer. It is to be sacrificed, burnt completely, and its ashes are to be mixed with fresh water. This compound is then used to purify those who come in contact with a dead body, yet those involved in its preparation become impure. This paradox has no logic and is therefore classified as a Hok, a law given by G-d that has no explanation. This is followed by the death of Moses' older sister, Miriam. Afterwards there is a severe water shortage eliciting a great outcry. G-d instructs Moses and Aaron to speak to a rock and it will produce water. Instead, Moses angrily strikes the rock. G-d rebukes both of them, and as punishment declares that neither Moses nor Aaron will enter the Promised Land. Moses asks permission from the King of Edom to pass through his land en route to Canaan and is rebuffed. Shortly thereafter Aaron dies and is succeeded by his son, Elazar, as high priest. The people again complain of the lack of water and the unsatisfying Manna. As punishment for their taunts of returning to Egypt, G-d sends fiery serpents to attack them. Moses again intercedes on their behalf by advising them to mount a brass serpent on a pole and those who look up to it will be saved. They resume their journey and are confronted by the army of Sihon, king of the Amorites, whom they defeat in battle. The Parshah concludes with the defeat of Og king of Bashan.

Excellence
versus Perfectionism

In previous *Parshiyot*, we see the gradual development of the Children of Israel from infancy as a new nation toward the goal of greater maturity. The Torah, with its built-in structure, is the guiding force in advancing their development as experienced during their sojourn in the wilderness. At this developmental stage, they are being presented with a strange mysterious rite which this week's *Parshat Hukkat* describes as a "statute." This Hebrew term (*Hukkat*) implies that it is a law whose rationale is not evident. The rite consists of slaughtering a "red heifer, faultless without blemish" (Num. 19:2). It is totally burned in fire, its ashes are mixed into a watery compound which is then used to purify those who have become defiled through contact with a dead body. To further the mystery, those who are involved in preparing the purifying ashes become impure, whereas the impure persons upon whom the red heifer compound is sprinkled become pure. The key Hebrew word referring to the red heifer is *temimah* (faultless), which means that it had to be perfectly red. Such an animal is obviously very rare, so why destroy it?

While cloaked in theological mystery, there is a psychological insight I would like to share about human behavior which may have relevance in illuminating this rite. The pursuit of perfectionism is an illusory goal which will ultimately turn into ashes, like the burning up of the perfectly red heifer. The realm of perfectionism belongs to the Almighty who created the red heifer, so it must be slaughtered and symbolically returned to its Maker. This is a lesson for the narcissistic personality who is driven by a compulsion to pursue self-glorification, or the perfectionist whose aspirations can never be fulfilled. Man can only strive to imitate G-d, *Imitatio Dei*, that is to reach a level of excellence through trial and error. When the center of the universe becomes oneself, and no one else is good enough, this is an illusion of perfectionism which can never be realized. The world then turns into a place of disillusionment, deprivation and disappointment. Therefore, the metaphor of the red heifer serves as an example that absolute perfection comes from G-d and returns to G-d. The slaughter of the red heifer and its death is also reminiscent of the very mystery of death itself, which like perfectionism, remains in the province of the Almighty.

To complete this metaphor, it is now understandable why those who are involved in the preparation of the red heifer (i.e. , perfectionism) are declared impure. Lest they think their exalted status entitles them to pursue perfectionism, they become impure. However, the masses who do not have priestly status and who are more subject to sin, may be sprinkled with the ashes of the once perfectly red heifer and become pure. On a psychological level this means that those who are involved with extreme narcissism either themselves or with others, invariably become damaged or muddied. Others who do not have the goals of perfectionism, who see themselves and their goals as realistic, and who strive for a better way of living can be helped symbolically by a sprinkling of "healthy narcissism" (the ashes). Healthy narcissism is being able to take care of oneself physically and psychologically. The healthy narcissist is one who has self-esteem based on reality and who strives to be the best he can be. Perfection is best left to G-d.

One of the great mysteries of Jewish history is the holocaust perpetrated by the Nazis which took the lives of six million Jews. There is no satisfying theological explanation that can justify such an unprecedented calamity. Perhaps the mystery of the red heifer can, however, offer some insight. The innocent victims of the Holocaust, in a remote sense, can be compared to the unblemished red heifer. In fact, Holocaust victims are often referred to as *korbanot*, the Hebrew word for "animal sacrifices," which were required to be *temimot*, "whole, unblemished. "Unfortunately, they, like the red heifer, were burned, but in the crematoria of the Nazi death camps. Their ashes have symbolically become the purifying agent for *Kelal Yisrael* (the totality of Israel); witness the miraculous establishment of the State of Israel following the Holocaust. The Nazis representing the perfection of the "master race" together with their willing allies were defeated, whereas the "subhuman" Jews cleansed by the purifying actions of their victimized brethren have emerged victorious. The souls of the innocent victims representing G-d's perfection have returned to their Maker carrying with them the eternal mystery of untimely death. Their brethren who survived the Holocaust, (many having sett led in Israel), are a shining example of what it means to become purified. Holocaust survivors, symbolizing the *Mayim Hayim*, (living waters), which were mixed with the ashes of the red heifer (i.e., the victims), together form the solution[2] which has the power to purify and become regenerated.

These survivors have rebuilt their lives and built new families from the ashes of the unspeakable physical horror and internal anguish to which they were subjected. Although we may never comprehend these mysteries, we are witnesses to miracles that followed these modern events, reminiscent of those experienced by the Israelites during their sojourn through the wilderness en route to the Promised Land. Today, against all odds, we are witnessing the remarkable achievements of the State of Israel, helped by the survivor generation and their descendants. This is the most profound statement of what it means to strive for excellence instead of the illusory superiority/perfection of the "master race."

---

2. How remarkable it is that the secret code term coined by the Nazis for the destruction of the Jewish people was the "Final Solution." This bears a mysical reference to the "solution," i.e., the living waters containing the ashes of the red heifer. From those ashes the secondary effect was the healing and growth of a new generation of Jews. The narcissistic pursuit of perfection inevitably destroyed Hitler and his racist collaborators.

Balak
Numbers 22:2-25:9
King Balak and the Soothsayer Balaam

Balak, king of Moab, fearing the advancing Israelites, dispatches a delegation to induce the soothsayer, Balaam, to curse the Israelites. After several entreaties, Balaam agrees to go to Balak. G-d dispatches an angel to block Balaam's way. Balaam's ass, seeing the angel on the road, stops and is beaten repeatedly by her master. A conversation ensues as the ass explains to Balaam why she cannot proceed. G-d reveals to Balaam the presence of the angel and reinforces the importance that Balaam say only what is told to him. After making elaborate preparations prior to cursing the Israelites, Balaam proceeds to compose beautiful prophecies about the great virtues of the Israelites, much to the consternation of King Balak. Notwithstanding Balaam's praises, the Israelites are subsequently seduced into worship of Baal-Peor, the god of the Moabites and Midianites. Zimri, a prince of the tribe of Simeon, publicly engages in a lewd act of idolatry with a Midianite princess in the presence of Moses. A plague breaks out as Divine punishment in which 24,000 sinners are killed. It ceases only after the intervention of Pinhas son of Elazar the high priest, who slays the offending couple.

The Power of Psychological Warfare

Commentary When we contrast the opening section of this week's Torah reading, *Balak* (King of Moab), with its conclusion, we see encapsulated a clever dual strategy employed by Balak to defeat the Israelites, who were encamped on his border. Balak realizes that he is powerless to overcome the Israelites in physical combat, so he resorts to psychological warfare. His strategy is to demoralize his opponent without having to "fire a single shot." Enter the pagan soothsayer, Balaam, who is engaged by Balak to curse the Israelite enemy. The strategy backfires, as Balaam, thanks to Divine intervention, utters some of the most beautiful prophetic praises of Israel ever recorded in the Torah.

Balak, undeterred, employs his second strategy in psychological warfare, consisting of temptation and seduction. This strategy succeeds as we read, "And they (Moabite women) called the people (Israelites) unto the sacrifices of their gods; and the people did eat, and bowed down to their gods. And Israel joined unto the Baal of Peor; and the anger of the Lord was kindled against Israel" (Num. 25:2-3). Israel is seduced into idol worship, a clear indication that even after forty years in the wilderness, they have again regressed to this childish stage of requiring a physical god as an object of worship and a loss of control over their impulses of lust and aggression.

As a result, G-d punishes them by sending a plague which kills 24,000 Israelites, more than Balak could ever have accomplished through conventional warfare. This relapse of Israel into idolatry of the Moabite god, Baal Peor, constitutes a victory for Balak despite the failure of his first strategy, that of Balaam's mission. It shows that the bitter lesson of worshiping the golden calf, which occurred at the outset of the Israelite forty year sojourn in the wilderness, has not been sufficiently learned. In psychological terms, the sin of Baal Peor is a regression to their childish Egyptian slave mentality of dependence and lack of integration of their newly acquired identity as an independent nation. Children are easily seduced by temptation, as they have not as yet developed self-control. The belief in an abstract unseen G-d, who rescues them from slavery and gives them the structure of Torah values, has not as yet fully penetrated into their consciousness.

People who have not established a firm inner identity will very often seek it externally by associating with those who appear successful. This kind of adopted group identity, as one sees in gangs and cults, is not secure, because it robs the individual of his independence, self-esteem and freedom of action. These people are not able to internalize their own set of values and ideals. Their identity fluctuates with the passing fads of society, which is a form of assimilation. The curse that Balaam could not articulate against the Hebrews was, however, acted out in the sin of Baal Peor. As regressed children, bereft of a new identity anchored in Torah values, they are easily seduced into assimilation with their idolatrous neighbors—the Moabites.

This bitter historic lesson is lamentably "alive and well" to this very day, especially in the *Galut* (Diaspora) where Jews are a minority seeking acceptance into the majority dominant culture. Historically, Israel has lost more souls through assimilation than through all the persecutions. The same struggle Moses endured in trying to strengthen the Israelites' newly won G-d-chosen identity against the allure and envy of the surrounding cultures is still being waged. When a sense of self is not secure, one looks to others to provide externally what is not accomplished internally. This accounts for the increasing level of intermarriage and assimilation occurring in the Diaspora Jewish community worldwide. Just like their ancestors in the wilderness, they are being enticed by their secular surroundings because they have lost their sense of self and separate identity. This is due, in no small measure, to their ignorance of that same Torah which their ancestors are struggling to internalize. The Torah, however, is more than a legal structure. It provides a model for developing maturity through psychological, ethical and moral growth. As we have seen, this model for internal identity and psychological growth is not acquired easily nor does it proceed in a straight line. The Israelites seem to take two steps forward only to be followed by taking one step backward, as in their relapse into idolatry and assimilation with the Moabites at the end of their long arduous journey.

Psychoanalysts Kohut and Winnicott have demonstrated the complexity of this process of developing a sense of self. It is only when the child reaches the stage of psychological maturity that the tendency toward compliance to another is overcome. Winnicott describes the "hidden self" as that remaining spark of the real self hidden by the cloak of a "false compliant self," because the child is not yet mature enough to handle life on his own. The child is in a state of compliance in order to win the approval and safety provided by his parents. When the child is, however, encouraged to develop his authentic hidden self and self-esteem, the need to win approval from the outside is no longer as compelling. This on-going growth process is reflected in all its difficult stages during the Israelites travels in the wilderness. They are now obviously frightened by the prospect of conquering the Canaanites. They regress into their compliant childhood selves, looking for safety through assimilation with others. The sin of Baal Peor demonstrates that assimilation is both a physical and psychological enemy. In the long term scheme of events, psychological warfare such as engineered by Balak and Balaam has proven to be more effective than physical combat. It is an ancient lesson that hearkens back to Biblical times with modern reverberations, which the infant Israelite nation will soon re-experience as they confront the Canaanites, et al, who occupy the Promised Land.

Pinhas
Numbers 25:10-30:1
The Second Census

*P*inhas, son of Elazar, and grandson of the High Priest, Aaron, earns the re- ward of hereditary High Priesthood by executing vengeance on Zimri and Cozbi who publicly profaned G-d's holy name. A second census is conducted because forty years had elapsed since the first census was taken after the exodus. This is done in order to determine the size of each of the tribes so that the amount of land apportioned to each tribe would be according to their respective populations. The five daughters of Zelophehad, from the tribe of Menasseh, raise an issue regarding inheritance of daughters when there are no sons. As a result of their successful petition, laws of inheritance are clarified. Moses is asked to ascend Mt. Abarim to view the Promised Land prior to his death. Joshua is appointed Moses' successor. A detailed description is given of the daily and festival offerings to take place in the Sanctuary after the conquest. A complete review of all the holy days, their dates and mode of observance is given.

The Art of Impulse Control

This week's Torah reading, *Pinhas* (Aaron's grandson), is a continuation of the previous *Parshah*, in that G-d is again testing whether the Israelites have internalized the laws of the Torah so that they are able to maintain their own identity in the face of temptation. Pinhas is the personification of the type of person who has internalized Torah values and has become his own "policeman." He is in stark contrast to the Baal Peor worshipers, who are easily seduced by the Moabite and Midianite women, because they had not as yet internalized Torah values. These values, while acknowledged, are still viewed as external laws which need to be carefully monitored and enforced by others. This issue runs throughout the *Parshiyot*, as G-d continually tests the Israelites' ability to be responsible for their own individual commitment regardless of what others do.

We see in this *Parshah* a contrast of impulse control between Pinhas and the Baal worshipers. Part of one's identity is how he deals with the internal impulses everyone has, not only in taming these impulses, but using them for whatever positive service they can provide. For example, a soldier's life may depend on his not restraining his murderous impulses during war time, but in ordinary life these impulses must be recognized and sublimated into positive assertiveness and protectiveness. Pinhas is able to direct his internal rage against the main perpetrators, thereby preventing others from joining Zimri and Cozbi in their lewd public idolatrous actions. The Baal worshipers, on the other hand, are unable to contain or redirect their sexual and lustful impulses without outside control. They are still subject to group psychology where they do whatever the group does and do not feel any individual responsibility for controlling their impulses.

Groups of violent people, directed towards a central goal, have the power to influence the individual to bypass one's super ego (i.e. conscience or moral control), in order to fulfill the group's objectives. Have we not seen people standing around and yelling "fight, fight" when others are being viciously attacked? We certainly have seen this in the Holocaust. Individuals who have a stronger more secure sense of self, who struggle with aggression, envy and lust will eventually succeed in gaining mastery over them and will be able to work cooperatively for the good. In Freudian terms this means, as repeated above, "to put ego where id was," that is, to tame impulses (not to be abstinent or not to feel), so that internal controls are able to master these recognized id impulses. G-d, through the Torah, is trying to create a people who can work together as a group, yet retain a sense of individual responsibility and commitment identified in Freudian term as ego and superego.

The saga of Moses learning to deal with his own anger, which is repeated throughout the history of his life, is also a reflection of the human condition. His leadership is geared towards helping his people grow individually through the Torah and to bond them as a group with clear boundaries and common goals. However, in this latest episode, when the Israelites lapse into licentious idolatrous rites, Moses is again being tested in his ability to control his impulses. In the face of the crisis at Baal Peor, which demands his immediate action, he again becomes paralyzed. He equivocates as he did at the *brit* of his son (see above *Parshat Shemot*), necessitating others to step in, e.g., Zipporah and Pinhas.

This is a display of his ongoing problem of when and where to express anger, e.g., breaking the *Luhot* (Ten Commandments) and striking the rock at Meribah. In each instance, he suffers the consequences of his volatile anger. Pinhas, on the other hand, who acts alone as an army of one, is able to channel his anger and murderous rage against the perpetrators, "And he [Pinhas] hath turned My wrath away from the Children of Israel, in that he was very zealous for My sake among them" (Num. 25:11). He is rewarded with the Divine promise about everlasting priesthood remaining in his family, unlike Moses, of whose descendants we know nothing.

The *Parshah* concludes with another example of zealotry being rewarded, but from a most unexpected quarter in those days—women. The five daughters of Zelophehad defy convention by going directly to Moses instead of to the lower courts to plead their case for the land rights of their deceased father in the absence of any male heirs. Moses addresses their petition directly to G-d, whose response is, "The daughters of Zelophehad speak right, thou shalt surely give them a possession of an inheritance among their father's brethren and thou shalt cause the inheritance of their father to pass unto them" (Num. 27:6).

This is a remarkable example of justice and equity for women in Judaism at a time when they were generally considered chattel by other nations. This Divine decision, favoring the daughters of Zelophehad, must have had a major psychological effect by increasing the self- esteem of Hebrew women and how they were viewed by the opposite sex. Is it any wonder that in the feminist movement in America, Jewish women were and are in the vanguard of leadership in securing justice for women? Whatever the case, whether in praising Pinhas, or in Moses acquiescing to the justice of inheritance rights for women, the Torah is implicitly counseling the Israelites about coping with various psychological issues, not the least of which is impulse control. In exhibiting appropriate impulse control, one reinforces a sense of internal power and mastery that fuels self-esteem which in turn enhances the ego. This power enabled Moses to overcome his internal "demons" allowing him to rise to unsurpassed leadership. It is this power and learned art of impulse control that Moses is constantly trying to exemplify for his people with limited success.

Mattot
Numbers 30:2-32:42
The Sacredness of Vows

*T*his Parshah discusses the sacredness of vows and the various procedures to be followed in making and annulling them. The Israelites engage the Midianites in battle in retaliation for their role in the sin of Baal-Peor, and are victorious by killing five Midianite kings and the soothsayer, Balaam. The tribes of Gad and Reuven petition Moses to remain East of the Jordan on conquered land deemed most suitable for their large livestock. While initially questioning their motives, Moses extracts a promise that the warriors in these tribes will participate in the conquest of Canaan and then return to their families East of the Jordan. Moses then proceeds to parcel out the land among the two and a half tribes.

"The Mind and the Body Meet at the Word"

The above aphorism, attributed to Dr. Sigmund Freud, points to the human distinction, in that man has a mind that develops and learns how to express itself in words, unlike the animal kingdom, which lacks the power of speech. The mind-body connection ties together the intellect with human physical drives so that man has the ability to be in charge of his physical needs. Accordingly, human psychological stresses are often expressed by physical symptoms such as headaches, high blood pressure, etc.

Our language emphasizes this strong mind-body connection in expressions such as, "he gives me a pain in the neck," or, "I feel my head will explode." These examples of psychogenic symptoms can be ameliorated according to Freud through the human gift of speech, "the word" (therapy), which can be utilized to manage and control the mind-body connection. Patients have told me that during therapy, when they feel safe to express their feelings, thoughts and fantasies, they have suffered fewer colds.

It is well known that excessive stress which has not been addressed can cause a breakdown in the immune system. The experience of therapy gives them relief from the need to constantly repress certain unwanted feelings. For example a patient remarked, "I used to be afraid to drive on the highway, but now I can" or, "my menstrual periods were always irregular, but now they are like clockwork." Often, these symptoms are not directly addressed in therapy, but disappear as a by-product of treatment. Words can heal, but words can also harm. During therapy, adults frequently remember the critical and traumatic statements made to them as children, such as "you are no good or crazy or nobody loves you," which are more painful than a knife. In giving vent to one's feelings during therapy, we see how the human asset of speech can successfully cope with the "fallout" of the mind-body connection.

A cogent example of Freud's insight into human behavior is found in this week's Torah reading *Mattot* (Tribes), which opens with a discussion of the subject of making vows. The vow is a verbal commitment to control one's inner physical and emotional states such as greed, envy, lust, aggression, etc. It is sometimes made in association with realizing an ideal, such as with Jacob, "And Jacob vowed a vow, saying, 'If G-d will be with me... I shall surely give a tenth unto thee'" (Gen. 28:20).

An example of a communal vow is recorded in this *Parshah*, as the tribes of Reuven, Gad and a half tribe of Menasseh vowed to join together with the other tribes in conquering the land West of the Jordan, providing they be granted the territory already conquered East of the Jordan. Moses extracts this vow to curb feelings of greed and personal gain on the part of these tribes at the expense of the other tribes. "And the land (Canaan) ye subdued before the Lord, and ye return afterward; then ye shall be clear before the Lord, and before Israel, and this land (East of the Jordan) shall be unto you for a possession before the Lord" (Num. 32:20-22). Although a vow entails making choices and behavioral options, it must observe certain boundaries and responsibilities in keeping with the terms of the vow.

The example of the vow taken by these tribes becomes a learning experience for all the tribes. It teaches them that outer physical conquest must be accompanied with the conquest of one's inner emotional drives. Similarly, in the vow one makes in the marriage ceremony, the physical union is accompanied by a vow, a verbal expression of responsibility and commitment to one's spouse. Therefore, the matter of annulling a vow must be made immediately (same day) because of the power of words in relation to the mind-body connection. The verbal vow, therefore, becomes an inner controlling force over behavior, as opposed to needing an external authority figure such as a parent or teacher. From a psychological perspective, a vow represents growth in terms of responsibility and commitment, key components in developing maturity.

From a religious standpoint, however, making a vow is frowned upon because at the conclusion of the period of the vow, one must bring a sin offering. This is discussed above in *Parshat Naso* regarding a Nazirite who separates himself from others by undertaking an ascetic regimen in order to devote himself totally to spiritual matters. The Nazirite vow is time limited, reinforcing the idea that the Torah does not recognize extended abstinence as a means of coping with internal issues at the expense of being part of the community. The Torah regards the maker of such a vow as distancing him/herself from others as was the case with the two and a half tribes. This is viewed as sinful, as the Torah ideal is developing self-control without the need of making a vow. The bringing of a sin offering is a means of assuaging guilt in having had to resort to making a religious vow. The expectation is that a vow will not be needed again in the future.

Although Freud, the arch secularist, had his own professional agenda in mind with his insights about the mind-body connection, it nevertheless has great relevance to psychological growth and development in the religious area as well. Accordingly, the Israelites are again receiving a subtle psychological message about self-awareness, impulse control and making informed voluntary choices within the context of community instead of outside of it.

Masei
Numbers 33:1-36:13
Wilderness Itinerary Review

*T*his being the last Parshah in the book of Numbers, the Torah
reviews the forty-two stations wherein the Israelites encamped
on their forty year journey from Egypt to Moab overlooking the
Jordan River. They are instructed to utterly destroy the Canaanites
and their idolatrous practices. Moses outlines the borders of the
Holy Land to be occupied by the twelve tribes according to their
respective populations. Since the tribe of Levi consecrated to the
service of G-d did not receive a contiguous portion of land, they are
to be distributed among all the tribes in forty-eight Levitical cities.
There are to be six cities of refuge, three each on either side of the
Jordan, designated for those guilty of involuntary manslaughter.
Moses addresses again the matter of inheritance rights for women
in families without male issue. The Parshah concludes the fourth
book of the Torah with the summarizing statement, "These are the
commandments and ordinances which the Lord commanded via
Moses unto the children of Israel in the plains of Moab by the Jordan
at Jericho" (Num. 36:13).

The Wilderness
Therapeutic Experience

This week's Torah reading, *Masei* (Journeys), which is usually combined with the previous week's reading *Mattot*, concludes the book of Numbers. It reviews the names of over forty stations where the Israelites encamped in their forty years of wandering in the wilderness, from Egypt to the Plains of Moab. As they are finally on the verge of entering the Promised Land, one wonders: is there nothing more momentous to discuss at this point than a routine "travelogue" of past encampments? Moreover, is there any contextual connection with its sister Torah reading of the previous week dealing with the subject of vows?

The answer to both questions is that there is an important psychological message that underscores both readings which needs to be recounted at this crucial juncture. The Israelites needed this extended journey in space and time in order to internalize G-d's value system as recorded in the Torah. It is a metaphor for G-d's saying, "Look how far you have come. See you have come from a dependent childlike state in Egypt unable to abstract an unseen G-d and unable to form a cohesive community. At this point, through the wilderness therapeutic experience, you have developed a non-Egyptian Israelite identity. Through the Torah, you now have a blueprint of boundaries and obligations which provide structure and safety for future growth and maturity." That is why the matter of vows is deferred to this point, because now they are ready to make vows which denote responsibility and commitment. In the relationship of the Israelites and G-d, there is a mutual commitment based on the Covenant between G-d and Abraham, the patriarch founder of the Chosen People. It is time now, on the doorstep of Canaan, to take stock and recapitulate the status of that Covenant.

We now see G-d's role not only as a spiritual guide, but G-d, as it were, the Therapist. The wilderness therapeutic experience has many parallels with what transpires in a therapeutic relationship. The areas that are brought up by the patient often reflect the redoing of the same issues over and over again, by looking at the same issues with new eyes. The territory covered may appear the same, but the patient is at a different psychological place that allows looking back with newer insights.

In this *Parshah*, Moses reviews for the people the physical territory they have traveled on their journey to psychological maturity. With the Torah blueprint for maturity as a guidebook, the metaphor is clear. Look how far you have traveled from dependency to autonomy, from slavery to productivity, from divisiveness to forming a united people, from concreteness of thinking and false idols to abstract thinking about an unseen G-d, from feeling inferior and helpless to having a strong personal and group identity. It is time now for G-d to review the therapeutic contract as well as the religious covenant. "Are you responsible enough to commit to and honor your end of the therapeutic contract? Can you commit to the therapeutic alliance?"

G-d states a new goal for the Israelites, "Ye shall drive out all inhabitants of the land before you, and destroy all their molten images and demolish all their high places for unto you have I given the land to possess" (Num. 33:52-53). This message is really not new, going to war means doing all of the above. G-d as therapist says in metaphor to his patient, "Look, we are now going into a new arena of yourself. You now see that I have given you an identity, a land and property that is to be yours. You now have to destroy all the old myths, models and mistakes of childhood and child-like behavior. This is your on-going task in the therapeutic alliance. If you can agree to participate in this struggle, I promise to give you new territory that is yours. When you empty yourself of the old childhood myths there is room to choose to internalize the new adult blueprint of maturity."

G-d, in the roles of Lord of Hosts and Therapist, brings the people into new territory with physical strength and emotional confidence needed to fulfill the terms of the Covenant. The strength of this contract will be further tested, as we come to the fifth and last book of the Torah, Deuteronomy.

THE BOOK OF DEUTERONOMY

"These are the words which Moses spake unto all Israel beyond
the Jordan; in the wilderness in the Arabah"
— *Deuteronomy* 1:1

Devarim
Deuteronomy 1:1-3:22
Moses' First Discourse

*T*he *fifth and last book in the Torah, Devarim, known as
Deuteronomy, is derived from the Greek word meaning
"repetition" or "review." In this book, Moses delivers several discourses
in which he rebukes the people for their sinful behavior prior to his
imminent death. In this Parshah, Moses delivers his first discourse in
which he reviews events occurring after Sinai on their way to Kadesh.
The weight of responsibility in leading such a large, fractious people
necessitates his establishing a judicial system as well as the election
of seventy elders to assist him. He laments the demoralizing report
presented by the twelve princely spies and the defeatist response of
the people. This leads to G-d's decision that the Egyptian-born adult
generation would die out in the wilderness, and that His covenant
would be carried out by the generations born in the wilderness.
Moses tracks their journey with flashbacks of what transpired in
various locations after leaving Kadesh. He recounts their victories
over Sihon and Og and the allotment of land east of the Jordan to
the tribes of Reuven, Gad and half tribe of Menasseh. Moses assures
his successor Joshua of his future success in conquest of Canaan with
G-d's help and not to be fearful.*

The Cycle of
Endings and Beginnings

It is not unusual with the coming of old age, that one begins to review past events as a way of reconciling a lifetime of accomplishments and failures. As we begin the last of the five books of the Torah, Moses at age 120 begins to review his life which is inextricably interwoven with his experiences with the people. He recounts in this *Parshah, Devarim* (Words) his first of three farewell discourses, the "ups and downs" of this relationship. This review, which covers the Israelites' forty year journey in the wilderness, is Moses' way of explaining in psychological terms, "How I became who I am." This corresponds with the review of the more than forty desert encampments listed in the previous *Parshah, Masei* which tells us how Israel coalesced into a nation.

While for Moses this review signals the end of "his story," it is an introduction for those born in the wilderness of a new life to begin for them in the Promised Land. Not yet knowing what their future will bring, they need to know "the history" of who they are and from whence they came.

In psychoanalytical terminology what Moses is doing in these final discourses is entering the "termination" phase of therapy. His recalling of the various encampments is more than just a review of geographic locations, but metaphorically, a way of reflecting on the different stages of his psychological and religious development. Moses has started the termination phase of his own therapy/

growth, with G-d, as it were, his therapist/mentor. His discourses are a way of Moses saying goodbye to his "Therapist" by implicitly detailing the steps of his development and growth from an earlier psychological stage where he was arrested. His review of events, difficulties and mistakes are all part of the therapeutic process of advancing through various psychological stages.

In the field of psychoanalysis there is a major schema detailing the human growth pattern which will help to better understand where the Israelites are now in their development toward maturity. This design was developed by psychoanalyst Eric Erikson, a student of Dr. Freud. Erikson identified eight stages in the life cycle of the individual from birth to death. An individual, who has to deal with trying circumstances as a child, may not be able to negotiate later stages as easily as someone who didn't have as many challenges early on.

For example, orphans who weren't held or stroked as infants have a hard time connecting with others when they become adults. The adolescent stage (12 to 18 years) stands out as the period when one begins to establish a personal identity. Up to this stage, according to Erikson, development depends primarily on what is done to us. From then on, development depends upon what we do. While an adolescent is neither a child nor yet an adult, life is getting more complex as he attempts to establish an identity and grapple with moral issues. In this process, it is common for adolescents to rebel and shirk responsibilities, since one does not have the backlog of experience in dealing with these issues.

The behavior of the Israelites during their wilderness therapeutic experience seems to place them in the adolescent stage in Erikson's schema of developmental stages. Being raised in the wilderness by parents who have a slave mentality and struggling for survival in difficult physical, social and emotional conditions, it is little wonder that Moses characterizes them as stiff-necked and rebellious. Struggling to adopt a new identity as G-d's chosen people, divesting themselves of a slave mentality, adapting themselves to being responsible to do things on their own rather than being told what to do, and then to developing a new ethical mode of behavior, they react to Moses their father-figure in typical adolescent defiant manner. Moses, the personification of the mature adult in Erikson's schema, recognizes the psychological realities of this adolescent stage by targeting in his final discourses their rebelliousness and moral shortcomings. Also characteristic of his stage of development (late adulthood 65 to death), Moses confronts his own failures in leadership. This is the psychological landscape that surrounds them as we open the book of Deuteronomy.

Va'ethanan
Deuteronomy 3:23-7:11
Moses' Second Discourse

*M*oses continues his first discourse by expressing his hope to enter the Promised Land, buoyed by his victories over the Amorite kings. He is, however, rebuffed, as G-d implores him not to raise this subject again. Moses is told that he may view the Promised Land from the heights of Moab, and that he should strengthen Joshua who is entrusted to carry out the conquest. Moses reminds them of their special status having experienced the revelation at Sinai. This seminal event is to be transmitted to their children throughout all generations. Moses reemphasizes the dangers of idolatry. He then assigns three cities of refuge to be located East of the Jordan.

Moses begins his second discourse by reviewing the religious foundations of G-d's covenant with the Israelites. In so doing, Moses repeats the Decalogue given at Sinai, especially for the generations born in the wilderness. This is followed by the declaration of Israel's faith in the oneness of G-d, known as the Shema. In observing these ideals and practices, they are forbidden to intermarry with the idolatrous Canaanite inhabitants. The Parshah concludes with Moses stating that the underlying principle behind these laws is to preserve their status as a holy people.

The Bridge between Hearing and Listening

In this week's Torah reading, *Parshat Va'ethanan* (Beseech), Moses continues to review events that transpired during their forty-year sojourn in the wilderness. He reemphasizes the unique experience of receiving the Ten Commandments on Mt. Sinai. This is followed by what has become the most distinctive phrase denoting the cardinal principle of Jewish faith, "Hear O Israel, the Lord our G-d, the Lord is one" (Deut. 6:4). Much has been written on the linguistic and theological interpretation of the six Hebrew words that comprise the *Shema* (Hear), which has become popularly known as the declaration or confession of Jewish faith.

As a psychoanalyst who is trained in the art of listening to my patients, this phrase has deep psychological and emotional significance. The command to "Hear O Israel" is more than just hearing, it is listening. Listening, in the therapeutic sense, represents an active rather than a passive stance. The psychoanalyst listener may be silent but the silence is active, taking in the conscious and unconscious meaning of the speaker's words. For example, in treating couples in marital distress, I have found that they really do not know each other, simply because they do not hear or listen to one another. This in turn leads to a breakdown of marital boundaries, resulting in lack of mutual respect and trust.

The main task of the therapist is to provide a setting in the consulting room that will counteract these negative forces. Firstly, the couple must learn about the importance of maintaining boundaries. This is exemplified in the consulting room by providing boundaries of safety consisting of complete confidentiality. Secondly, listening to one another is modeled in the serious manner by which the therapist listens to them before venturing to interpret their problems. The main objective is getting each member of the couple to really know his/her partner. This can be accomplished by eliciting a new way of listening to one's partner with renewed respect and by restoring appropriate boundaries. When each partner learns the other's needs and they decide together how to meet them, the marriage can then begin to restore the desired functioning and caring.

This therapeutic alliance formed between the therapist and the patient in some ways parallels the desired bond sought between G-d and Israel. If Israel is willing to truly listen and hear G-d's voice as expressed in the Shema, then there can be a loving and productive relationship. How one begins to form this bond is immediately addressed in the paragraph following the *Shema*, "Thou shalt love the Lord thy G-d with all thy heart, with all thy soul and with all thy might" (Deut. 6:5). This love is to be taught and transmitted to each succeeding generation. "Thou shalt teach them [the words of Torah] diligently unto thy children and shalt talk of them when thou sittest in thy house and when thou walkest by the way, and when thou liest down and when thou risest up" (Deut. 6:7). Parents are supposed to be active role models who consciously promote continuity by educating their children to study Torah and observe its laws. This is what is meant by listening which gets translated into an action program of commitment. This paragraph of the *Shema* (Deut. 6:4-9) becomes a shorthand blueprint of what it means to love G-d.

An echo of this approach of loving G-d is found in Erich Fromm's book, *The Art of Loving*. Fromm, a psychoanalyst, defines love of one's mate as consisting of four components: knowing, respecting, caring and doing. The implication is that we cannot truly love someone we do not know or respect. Caring about one's mate in Fromm's view is not just a matter of emotion and romantic love, but involves doing that which pleases the mate. This definition of the characteristics of human love helps explain how one can love G-d. It involves the same basic four ingredients: knowing and respecting His will as expressed in the Torah; caring and doing by committing oneself to Torah observance. In reciting the *Shema*, it is a call for the full range of commitment, from the superficial external "hearing," to listening to the deeper psychological meaning of what lies beneath this verbal confession of faith.

Moses, in his last moments on earth, wants assurance in their reciting the *Shema* that they overcome their adolescent rebelliousness, and not lose sight of the higher more mature religious goals set before them for all generations by their loving heavenly Father.

Ekev
Deuteronomy 7:12-11:25
Lessons of the Wilderness

*M*oses continues his second discourse by promising blessings in their new land through obedience to the Torah. The land of Israel will be blessed with seven types of produce: wheat, barley, grapes, figs, pomegranates, olives, and date-honey. They are cautioned against self-glorification when enjoying these G-d-given blessings. In his historical musings, Moses reminds them of the sin of the golden calf and his need to ascend Mt. Sinai again to bring down a second set of the Tablets. To overcome the Israelite penchant for rebelliousness and resulting punishment, Moses returns to the theme of Shema, with its call for obedience and accompanying rewards. The land will then yield its produce accompanied by bountiful rain, and the surrounding enemies will be defeated.

Moses and Israel:
A Model for Marriage?

O ften couples come into my office with issues concerning a
troubled marriage. It is hard to get them past the emotional
wounding of not being loved, or of their feeling that the original
contract (spoken or unspoken) has been broken, leaving the
partners full of anger and hurt. Invariably, the issues presented in
the marriage are not from the marriage alone, but are psychological
problems stemming from growing up in their respective families.
If they can remember from where they came, and resolve some
of their growing up and maturation problems, the chances of
dealing successfully with marital difficulties are greatly improved.
The marriage contract then becomes a commitment between two
adult partners, rather than a battleground for resolving unresolved
pre-marital personal issues.

When we view Moses' farewell recounting of issues between
himself as G-d's chosen one and the Children of Israel within the
theoretical construct of a marriage relationship, we can see the
emergence of prior unresolved psychological issues. In this week's
Torah portion *Ekev* (Because), Moses exhorts them to remember
the lessons they have learned in growing up in the wilderness,
"And thou shalt remember all the way which the Lord thy G-d hath
led thee these forty years in the wilderness, so He afflicted thee, to
prove thee, to know what was in thy heart, whether thou wouldst
keep His commandments or no" (Deut. 8:2). Their behavior

is akin to that of children learning how to grow up and assume responsibilities. Therefore, they need to be disciplined. Moses is cast into the parental role with the unenviable task of serving as G-d's representative in administering the necessary *Musar* (exhortation), "And thou shalt consider in thy heart that as a man chastises his son, so the Lord thy G-d chastises thee" (Deut. 8:5).

The psychoanalytical principle of "transference" is operating throughout Moses' reminding the Children of Israel of what has transpired, as well as their looking forward now to entering the Promised Land. Transference is the state whereby the person unconsciously experiences another person as an earlier, usually unresolved parental figure. In the marriage state for example, one partner may reenact with the other as if he/she were the neglectful, overbearing or extremely loving parent. In other words, they are unable to see their partner as a separate individual who interacts in a way different than the transferential parental figure would react.

Moses, in addressing the people, is experiencing his own transference reaction. He sees them as abandoning him in difficult times in much the way he felt abandoned by his parents as an infant, rather than seeing the people as regressed, infantile and needing someone constantly to sustain and nurture them. His rage when striking the rock instead of speaking to it, is an example of Moses' anger that G-d now also has abandoned him as the people had done to him at the golden calf.

It is therefore necessary for Moses to overcome his transference reaction, working through with the people in his discourses all of his earlier experiences, as married couples do in psychotherapy. In so doing, they begin to see each other in a different light that enables the healing process to proceed. In assuming their new adult roles in eye-shot of their final objective, the Israelites need to view their lives with a changed perspective. Moses therefore cautions them, "Lest thou say in thy heart, my power and the might of my hand hath gotten me this far, you must remember the Lord thy G-d hath given thee this power in order that He may establish His covenant which He swore unto thy fathers" (Deut. 8:17-18). The underlying bonding of this new relationship is a mature recognition of the covenantal relationship between the Children of Israel and the One G-d of Israel. In speaking to them, Moses is also speaking to himself, by working through his own transference issues. These last discourses to the people are proving to be a catharsis for Moses himself in finding solace and internal peace in his final moments.

Re'eh

Deuteronomy 11:26-16:17

Rehearsal of the Code

In this Parshah, Moses projects the destiny of the nation to be dependent upon each individual's ability of making the right choice between two alternatives. Blessings will accrue when choosing to observe G-d's law, and curses will result when turning away from it. Moses then proceeds to review laws concerning the Mishkan, the central Sanctuary, laws against idolatrous rites, laws concerning bringing of tithes and first fruits, and a review of laws relating to the Three Pilgrimage Festivals. Private altars are prohibited once a sanctuary is built in Israel. Unlike in their travels in the wilderness, meat for food may be eaten anywhere in Israel. Procedures are stated for recognizing and coping with false prophets and religious seducers. Moses reminds them about observing the dietary laws a prerequisite for being a holy nation. Procedures to be followed during the Sabbatical year are restated and amplified. Special provision is made during the third and sixth years within the Sabbatical cycle for tithes to be given to the poor. A Hebrew bondsman is to be released after six years of servitude. If he chooses to remain enslaved, his ear is to be pierced and is released in the Jubilee year. A complete review of each of the Three Pilgrimage Festivals—Pesach, Shavuoth and Sukkoth concludes this Parshah.

Torah Mathematics

In this *Parshah, Re'eh* (See), Moses concludes his review of historical events and begins to highlight laws dealing with governance, torts, domestic life and holiday observances. Some commentators say that this *Parshah* could loosely be considered an expansion of the Decalogue. Because of the wide range of material covered by Moses in this discourse, one may not feel the impact of a major caveat, which states, "All this that I command you that ye shall observe to do; thou shalt not add thereto, nor subtract from it" (Deut. 13:1). Moses is warning them about Torah "math," which has psychological implications.

One may not add laws to the Torah as a pretentious exhibition of religiosity or grandiosity, nor subtract from it as a way of breaking the wholeness and unity of this structured system. This system, which is of Divine origin, is now passing on to human administration and interpretation. Human beings are blessed with free will and have the power to interpret the Torah. This blessing of free will is counter-balanced by accepting responsibility for human decisions, which can end up as a blessing or as a curse.

This trade-off is enunciated in the opening passage of this *Parshah*, "Behold, I set before you this day a blessing and a curse. This blessing is ye shall hearken unto the commandments of the Lord... and the curse, if ye shall not hearken unto the commandments of the Lord your G-d" (Deut. 11:26-28).

Moses is conveying an important psychological message, that individual and community maturity entail making difficult life choices. This ability to make choices was denied you in your dependent enslaved existence in Egypt which kept you in your infantile state. Now that you have that ability, do not abuse it either by adding to it or by subtracting from it. The motivation for its possible abuse is targeted by Moses as coming from the impact of surrounding cultures.

An example cited by Moses of "poor addition" is the unwise choice of the bondsman to remain enslaved after his period of servitude is concluded. This choice is an aberration, as it is a throwback to immature Egyptian dependency. The bondsman is therefore "earmarked" as a sign that he is unable to become an independent person.

Another example of "poor addition" is the bereaved person who elects to add on the mourning customs of neighboring nations by disfiguring oneself. It also "subtracts" from the Torah's method of bereavement which is an emotional psychological process of how to experience grief, rather than inflicting physical punishment. Underlying these examples is the Torah's sensitivity to the importance of identity, knowing who you are and where you come from. It is the insecure person who tries to take on the false identity of someone else, rather than choosing and struggling to experience the beauty of one's own identity and culture.

Moses' message of Torah addition and subtraction is lamentably as relevant today as it was in Biblical times. We see it in a recent trend within religious circles where new *humrot* (restrictions) are being added involving the separation of the sexes. In the past, this traditional separation of the sexes existed primarily at religious services, but recently it has expanded into educational and social gatherings. The *mehitzah* (barrier) traditionally reserved to separate the sexes at services, has made its appearance on the dance floor to further separate the sexes during wedding dances.

Other examples could be cited of this trend toward adding *humrot*. While these may be well intended because of maintaining *tzniyut* (modesty), they, nevertheless, run counter to the spirit of Moses' admonition of addition as well as of subtraction. Just as Moses reminds the individual to choose wisely, so in modern times the community-at-large, like its ancestors of old, must exercise restraint and discretion in how it expresses its zeal of commitment to Torah ethics.

Shoftim
Deuteronomy 16:18-21:9
Judges and Justice

*T*he impartiality of judges (shoftim), a paramount principle in
dispensing judgment, is Moses' opening message in this Parshah.
*A high court, later to be known as the Sanhedrin, is to be established
in the central Sanctuary which will arbitrate difficult cases beyond
the purview of the lower courts.*

*The selection, qualifications and duties of a king are set forth.
He is not to be above the law and is subject to certain restrictions
to prevent this from happening. As a constant reminder of his role,
a copy of the Torah law must accompany him at all times. The
priests and Levites who receive no land as an inheritance are to be
supported by the other tribes through a system of tithes. G-d will
inspire true prophets to guide the people to carry out His will. With
regard to criminal law, Moses refers again to the cities of refuge,
strictures are instituted against removing boundary markers and
ways of screening witnesses are provided. In waging war, the priest
as religious leader is directly involved, certain individuals are
exempt, fruit trees are not to be destroyed and offers of peace are to
be made prior to attacking. The Parshah concludes with a special
procedure to be followed by the elders, when an unclaimed body is
found between two cities.*

Who are the Real Judges?

In this Parshah, *Shoftim* (Judges), Moses directs his attention to the judicial system, admonishing the judges to be scrupulously honest in adjudicating matters coming before them, "Thou shalt not distort judgment, thou shalt not respect persons; neither shalt thou take a gift; for a gift doth blind the eyes of the wise and pervert the words of the righteous" (Deut. 16:19).

Here too is an underlying psychological component in dispensing justice. The judges must be willing to see the truth and not be blinded by personal considerations. Whereas this charge is directed to judges, it applies as well to each individual. The requirement is to see what you see, the reality, and not what you would like to see. We often defend ourselves against seeing what is too traumatic, uncomfortable and what may not fit into our vision of people, politics or religion. In order to make ourselves more comfortable with the status quo, we repress or deny what we really see so that change and growth cannot take place. This provides an excuse to escape from responsibility, because I am not obligated to do anything as it doesn't exist for me. It is a way of self-deception which is a form of dishonesty. We then lose the ability to stretch our minds to a higher level and open our eyes to new challenges and choices.

This was revealed to me in treating some patients from the ultra-orthodox community. They reported unwillingness by their leadership to see increasing signs of drug abuse, pedophilia, spousal abuse, adultery, homosexuality, etc. They were being blinded by their conviction that these are forbidden to Torah observant Jews, ergo non-existent. If the problem did not exist, then denial removed the responsibility to correct it. (More recently, however, there have been the beginning signs of a "clearing of the eyes" as educational programs have been undertaken to address some of these abuses.)

Many years ago a patient I had in therapy would become very excited whenever he acquired something of substantial monetary value. He felt that with the acquisition of wealth, he would finally have importance and could feel better about himself. Later on in analysis, he recounted to me the following dream. "I was in some kind of cave or dirty tunnel. My mother was there and she threw this mucky, filthy dirt in my eyes." His associations in the dream went to his feelings of lack of self worth, feeling dirty, worthless and having no value.

His abusive mother projected all of her failings on him, claiming that because he was so awful, she was the way she was. The only thing that would make his mother happy was attaining the status of being wealthy by "hook or crook." The patient "costumed" himself into being the bad unworthy child in order to relieve the mother of her guilt in abusing her son. Safety meant seeing the world through the distorted vision of his mother's eyes. The only possible restitution for self-worth and self-esteem was through accumulating money or obtaining valuable objects. He could not dare to deal with the world in an objective light and to see what was really important in his own abilities and character. According to the dream, his mother threw dirt into his eyes, which prevented him from seeing himself as he really was or the world as it really is.

In addressing the judges, Moses is really discussing the responsibility of leadership in general, to see what they see in order to deal with it. They should not allow their eyes to be clouded by fear of not being loved or by their own past experiences, but to be scrupulously honest and objective. This is a heavy burdensome responsibility open only to those leaders and judges of the highest character. What this *Parshah* is teaching us is an important psychological lesson. Not seeing reality is a way of keeping ourselves inept and immature by our unwillingness to accept responsibility for change. Outward religiosity and observance, should not blind us from seeing internal problems where they exist and attend to them. Who are the real judges? Not just the legally appointed experts, but each person who must engage in introspection and be willing to make the adjustments necessary to correct his flaws. Moses reviews some of the Torah laws to guide the Israelites in making the right choices. He may just as well be speaking to us today.

Ki Tetzei

Deuteronomy 21:10-25:19

Miscellaneous Laws

Continuing with the theme of the previous Parshah concerning waging war, Moses instructs the people about procedures to be followed with a female captive. She must be treated humanely, and after a month she is either to remain a concubine or released but not sold into slavery. Procedures are given when an incorrigible son is brought by his parents for trial before the elders. Miscellaneous laws of kindness are given, concerning restoring lost objects, proper burial of executed criminals, erecting parapets on rooftops, kindness to mother birds and animals, considerate treatment for employees and runaway slaves. Laws governing the institution of marriage and divorce, violations of engagement and marriage vows, immodesty and other forms of immorality are discussed. The holiness of the camp is to be preserved through proper sanitation and avoidance of personal and moral pollution.

Other miscellaneous laws refer to: Tzitzit—fringes worn on four cornered garments, avoidance of wearing mingled fabrics—shaatnez, fraternal lending without profit, taking and restoring a pledge, avoidance of usury, avoidance of excessive punishment of criminals and the importance of having honest weights and measures. The Parshah concludes this overview of so many regulations based on the principles of justice and brotherly love, with Moses' admonishment never to forget what the cowardly Amalekites did when they departed from Egypt.

The Torah's
Mini Psychoanalysis

One may wonder why this *Parshah*, *Ki Tetzei* ("when thou goest forth" [to battle]), contains the greatest number of Mitzvoth (commandments), seventy-four, more than any other *Parshah* in the Torah. Is there any common thread between all of these various commandments that could unite them together?

There is a common denominator, if we analyze them from a psychological perspective. The unifying bond is using the strictures of law to control man's inner impulses and desires. The natural unconscious desire of man is to take what he wants when he wants it without regard for others, especially from those who are weaker than he. The Torah, being sensitive to human nature, is setting up ethical ground rules to guide mankind in his sexual, social, financial and interpersonal relationships.

It is interesting to note that among all of the six hundred and thirteen commandments listed in the Torah, there is no prohibition against eating rocks. This is due to the fact that humans have no desire to do so. However, in this *Parshah* we do find concern that humans have a natural desire to exploit the weaker sex, animals, slaves, etc., ergo the need for legislation.

The guiding principle behind this diverse legislation is establishing a standard for justice and equality which is reflected in these commandments. The Torah recognizes that we all have temptations and that we may not be self-motivated to pursue justice and righteousness. Many people are still in the stages of learning how to do this and some may fail. This *Parshah* is supplying many road signs giving us direction towards reaching maturity and toward making moral decisions. There is also a clear statement against self-deception and outright negation of these Mitzvoth, in stating that, "For all who commit these infractions, they are an abomination to the Lord, those who do unrighteously..." (Deut. 25:16).

The *Parshah* concludes with a commandment which appears to contradict the standard of justice, compassion and equality set above, "When the Lord thy G-d hath given thee rest from all thine enemies round about, in the land which the Lord thy G-d giveth thee for an inheritance to possess it, that thou shalt blot out the remembrance of Amalek from under heaven; thou shalt not forget" (Deut. 25:19). Where is the feeling of compassion and the importance to act justly?

Anticipating this caveat, the Torah explains, "Remember what Amalek did unto thee on the road when ye came forth from Egypt; how he met thee on the road and smote the hindmost of thee, all that were enfeebled in thy rear, when they were faint and weary; and he feared not G-d" (Deut. 25:17, 19). The Torah is qualifying its concern for justice and compassion by excluding a nation that personifies the very antithesis of Torah values. Amalek crossed the line of basic humanity by its cowardly attack against the weak and defenseless. Therefore, they are not entitled to the humane concerns that underlie a civilized society. Amalek, like their spiritual descendants, Nazi Germany, earned the eternal enmity of G-d and the Jewish People.

There is another side to Amalek which lies beneath the surface making it difficult to detect, hence even more dangerous. Amalek is not only the external enemy that threatens one's physical existence, but he is an internal enemy that threatens one's psychological welfare. Amalek is representative of unconscious drives and impulses which left unchecked will destroy an individual and those around him.

All of this *Parshah*'s laws are addressed to Israel to do battle on two fronts. The Torah begins with miscellaneous laws such as coping with a rebellious son, restoring lost property, building parapets on rooftops, sparing a mother bird, laws against incest and adultery, etc. These laws are also designed to control unconscious impulses of aggression, greed, lust, selfishness, etc. Through these laws G-d is saying that one should be aware of these impulses which border on the animalistic—making you like Amalek, out of control. This does not mean an allowance for passivity.

Therefore, the *Parshah* concludes with dealing forcefully with Amalek. If someone is out to destroy you physically, use force to protect your people and religion, however, do not allow yourself to forget the destructive Amalek forces inside of you.

In this *Parshah* G-d is showing us that He recognizes the unconscious, i.e., the hidden baser impulses of humankind, by making them conscious through enacting appropriate commandments to curb them. These commandments are really implementing a form of mini-psychoanalysis, each teaching us the art of preventative therapy, by observing commandments that address the primitive unknown parts of the human psyche.

Ki Tavo
Deuteronomy 26:1-29:8
Making the Correct Choices

*M*oses concludes his Second Discourse by discussing the prayer and rituals that will accompany the presentation of first fruits to the priest and the tithes to the Levites and the poor in the Promised Land. This thanksgiving prayer for the first fruits includes a brief historical account of the Egyptian saga, leading up to G-d's key role in bringing them to the Promised Land. Moses' Third Discourse opens with instructions to follow after crossing the Jordan, especially reaffirming their commitment to the Torah. This is to be symbolized by erecting a stone altar, and inscribing words of the Torah on large stones. To dramatize the importance of making the correct choices in obeying G-d's law, the twelve tribes are to be divided six and six onto Mt Gerizim and Mt Ebal. The Levites stationed in the valley between them, are to recite a litany of blessings and mostly curses, to which in antiphonal cadence those on the mountains answer "Amen". At its conclusion, Moses sums up the entire Egyptian experience followed by their forty year wanderings in the wilderness, by cautioning them again that obedience to the Torah is the only way that will bring success in their new land.

A National Psychodrama

This *Parshah*, *Ki Tavo* ("When you come" [into the Promised Land]), is memorable because of its detailed graphic description of the *tochachah* (admonishment), a list of terrible consequences to befall Israel if they choose to disobey G-d's law. This theme, which was introduced earlier (Lev. 26:14-45), is highlighted here again in expanded form as they are on the verge of entering the Promised Land. This admonishment is counterbalanced by a much smaller listing of blessings that would accrue if Israel chooses to obey G-d's law. Why the great disparity in favor of punishment for sin, over the prospect of Israel's choosing to opt for morality and blessing? Furthermore, why the theatrics? To drive home the consequences of their behavior pro or con, Moses proposes a future mass dramatic scenario upon their entering the Promised Land. He divides the twelve tribes in half, by placing six tribes on Mt. Gerizim and the other six tribes atop Mt Ebal. He then stations his tribe of Levi in the valley between them. The Levites are instructed to turn to those tribes assembled on Mt. Gerizim and pronounce G-d's blessings, to which they answer "Amen." They then turn to those tribes on Mt. Ebal and deliver the Tochachah, to which they too answer "Amen." What is driving Moses in his last dying days to propose this uncharacteristic dramatic production?

In probing Moses' motivation, we may again benefit from psychological experience. This dramatic technique proposed by Moses is familiar to us today as psychodrama. The purpose of this massive "mountain psychodrama" is to engage all of the assembled in vicariously experiencing the possible consequences of the choices they make in the future, instead of their being passive spectators listening to another of Moses' exhortations. This dramatic scenario involves all of their senses in order to make a lasting impression in a very personal way. Whatever vestige of Egyptian slavery mentality, immorality and idolatry that remains after forty years in the wilderness needs now to be expunged, so Moses in desperation resorts to proposing this remarkable psychodrama.

This psycho-dramatic experience also helps explain the need for excessive warnings of punishment for disobeying G-d's commandments. As a newborn nation in the early stages of their moral development, the Israelites are akin to young children who are tempted to touch fire without realizing the consequences. Sometimes the best means of censure is a repeated slap on the wrist until they get the message. This psychodrama is Moses' strategy of choice to convince his young rebellious flock of what the stakes are in their future home in Canaan. It is also an attempt to mobilize all of the tribes facing one another, so they begin to feel what it means to be part of one large family. In order to overcome the enemy and all of the challenges of settling in a new land, the tribes must recognize they are part of the greater Israelite family and should act accordingly.

We know today, thanks to studies in family dynamics, how to differentiate between healthy and dysfunctional families. The family is a system of interlocking and interdependent relationships. There is a growth and life cycle pattern which unfolds within the family structure. Change and growth creates dilemmas and new solutions. In the dysfunctional family, the life cycle will engender dilemmas that promote dysfunction, disturbance, delinquency and other forms of disharmony. Witness the episodes involving Esau and Jacob growing up in the household of Isaac and Rebeccah.

Moses begins to explain the mechanics of a harmonious family, which comes about with open communication and a clear working out of rules and relationships based on the Divine Covenant. The terms of the Covenant are spelled out dramatically on the two mountain tops to which the people answer "Amen."

This means that they have chosen to work within the terms of the Covenant. However, Moses admonishes them, if they continue to be dysfunctional and defy the terms of the Covenant; then they will bring the *tochachah* upon themselves.

This scenario is not unlike what transpires in the therapist-patient agreement for treatment. It is not an equal relationship, as the ground rules are set by the therapist. If the patient consents to treatment and adheres to certain boundaries, the process begins. The patient learns to look inside at personal impulses in order to gain control over them, or chooses to stay within familiar childlike behavior and suffer continued dysfunction. This Parshah expresses in dramatic, graphic Biblical terms what often transpires in the consulting room regarding the requisites for a successful marriage and healthy family life. Moses reminds the people that they have heard the terms of being part of the Israelite family, and they must now choose the path that predicts the outcome. Unfortunately his dwelling on the Tochachah proves prophetic, once the Israelites are settled among the idolatrous Canaanites.

Netzavim
Deuteronomy 29:9-30:20
G-d's Eternal Covenant

*T*his short Parshah finds all of the people, Netzavim (standing), prepared to hear Moses' last words prior to his death. He declares that the Covenant not only binds them, but all future generations. He concludes this Third Discourse by stressing the importance of repentance. Although ultimately driven into exile, sincere repentance will result in the in-gathering of the exiles. Moses assures the people that His Torah is not distant, that it is not in the heavens or beyond the sea, but it is nearby and accessible. As you are about to cross the Jordan, you have free will to choose that which will bring blessings or curses. Choose life, which means to love G-d and observe His Torah. This is the fulfillment of the Covenant entered into between G-d and the patriarchs—Abraham, Isaac and Jacob.

A Covenant with
G-d is an Eternal Contract

One of the struggles that we all encounter in going up the developmental ladder is the issue of commitment. As very young children, the commitment is one-sided, from parent to child. Upon reaching Bar/Bat Mitzvah age, one begins the journey of learning to struggle with aspects of owning personal commitment and responsibility. For many this becomes a life-long struggle.

In this *Parshah*, Moses reminds the Israelites of the *Brit*, "Covenant," with the Almighty entered into by the patriarchs. This Covenant is more than the usual contract, as it binds together G-d and the Jewish people for all time. "Neither with you only do I make this Covenant and this oath, but with him that standeth here with us this day before the Lord our G-d, and also with him that is not here with us this day" (Deut. 29:13-14).

In initiating a contract, you usually have two consenting parties committed to carrying out the terms of the contract. If, however, one of the partners to the contract is authoritarian, who can do everything, and the other is totally subservient and incapable of autonomous action, then this is an unfair contract between an adult and a minor. Clearly this is not what G-d intended in choosing Abraham to partner with Him in establishing the Covenant. He wanted an autonomous mature adult who could commit himself and future generations in carrying out the terms of the contract. To emphasize this point, Moses waxes poetic in describing the accessibility of the Covenant, "For this commandment which I command thee this day, it is not too hard for thee, neither is it too far away. It is not in heaven, that thou shouldst say, 'Who shall go up for us to heaven, and bring it unto us, and make us hear it, that we may do it?' Neither is it beyond the sea, that thou shouldst say, 'Who shall go over the sea for us, and bring it unto us, and make us hear it, that we may do it?' But the word is very nigh unto thee, in thy mouth, and in thy heart, that thou mayest do it" (Deut. 30:11-14). Moses is stressing the fact that the Torah is not esoteric, but "down to earth." It, however, involves a personal commitment that no one else can do for you. The problem is that commitment to others and especially to a Higher Being is a stage of adulthood that many of the recently freed slaves have not yet reached.

The difficulties Moses is experiencing with the Children of Israel in developing a sense of commitment is not unlike this issue as it pertains to adults and children. The way an adult commits and the way a child commits are entirely different. A child at the dependency versus autonomy stage of development (see Eric Erikson), commits only to his immediate needs and does not experience anyone else's needs.

An autonomous adult, who has moved into the appropriate stages of adulthood, not only can commit to others, but can recognize other higher forces in life to which he may owe a commitment. The dependent child in his infantile narcissism says, "It's all about me and meeting my needs." As we grow older and relinquish some of this narcissism in favor of a more worldly outlook, we realize that we also have power to make things happen. The range of our commitment is expanded as is our ability to fulfill these commitments. This adult type persona, personified by Moses, is what G-d is grooming the Israelites in the wilderness for forty years, otherwise He could have done it all Himself, and they would have followed blindly along as in the stages of infantile dependency. This is the reason why Moses wants all of the assembled Israelites to renew the Covenant, in adult fashion, at this particular time prior to his impending death.

In my experience, this issue of commitment is frequently played out during marital therapy. In a good marital relationship, fidelity and commitment are directed to each other. In a dysfunctional marriage, the commitment is misdirected from one another to anyone of the fol- lowing: family of origin, oneself only, to outsiders or to one's career.

By contrast, Moses is attempting to direct the Israelites sense of commitment to fulfilling the terms of the Covenant. They saw in the patriarch Abraham a role model of supreme commitment to G-d through his own circumcision and through the *Akeidah* of his son Isaac. Moses' leadership in the exodus, revelation at Sinai and guiding them through the wilderness are testaments of his deep abiding commitment to G-d. Now Moses is saying this is how commitment to the Covenant works. G-d followed through on His commitment by taking the Israelites out of Egypt, by giving them the Torah and promising them a land flowing with milk and honey. Now it is time for the Israelites to follow the example of the patriarchs by embracing the Torah and becoming a unified family. The Torah is accessible to everyone. It is now up to the people to fulfill their part of the Covenant.

Vayelech

Deuteronomy 31:1-31:30

Moses' Last Days

*M*oses laments that his leadership is about to end at age 120 and that Joshua with G-d's help will lead them into the Promised Land. He exhorts Joshua to be strong and courageous. To make the Torah more accessible, Moses declares that every seven years during the Sukkoth festival, all Israel should assemble at the central Sanctuary to hear the king read portions of the Torah. Moses and Joshua are summoned into the Tent of Meeting, where G-d reveals that the Israelites will prove to be unfaithful to Him. He instructs them to write a ballad – Ha'azinu (next Parshah) to serve as a "witness" against their unfaithfulness. Moses completes his transcription of the Torah which is to be placed beside the Tablets in the Holy Ark.

The Ever Present Danger of Assimilation

This short *Parshah*, *Vayelech* (And he [Moses] went), is a continuation of the previous one (*Netzavim*), which are usually read together on the same Sabbath. It adds further closure to Moses' life as it states, "Behold thou [Moses] art about to sleep with thy fathers; and this people will rise up, and go astray after the foreign gods of the land, whither they go to be among them, and will forsake Me, and break My Covenant which I have made with them" (Deut. 31:16). The level of mature commitment to the Covenant which Moses expects of all the assembled, as discussed above, is obviously premature. Nevertheless, G-d keeps His end of the Covenant by reaffirming that they will enter the Promised Land. The *Parshah* concludes with Moses reinforcing G-d's ominous forecast by declaring, "For I know that after my death, ye will deal corruptly, and turn aside from the way which I have commanded you, and evil will befall you in the end of days" (Deut. 31:29).

This concluding ominous forecast of Israel's backsliding when exposed to foreign cultures, is true in our times as well. It is called assimilation, the antithesis of Israel's Biblical role as an *am kadosh*, a holy people who would be separate and different. Assimilation (as op- posed to acculturation), leads to the loss of one's true inner identity, which may have serious psychological repercussions.

For example as secular and anti-religious as Dr. Sigmund Freud was, he never changed his Jewish identity. In fact, it was reported that he counseled a male Jewish analytic patient to circumcise his newborn son contrary to the wishes of the secular father. He is reputed to have said, "You have no right to rob your son of his identity." Freud's reasoning was based on sound psychological grounds of maintaining one's identity, rather than on having his patient fulfill this as a religious obligation. Freud apparently also recognized that circumcision (Hebrew, *brit*) means "covenant," so that in observing this ritual one enters the covenant (*bnai brit*) which has become the mark of Jewish identity as stated, "And G-d said unto Abraham, 'And as for thee, thou shalt keep My Covenant, thou and thy seed after thee throughout their generations.... Every male among you shall be circumcised... and it shall be a token of a Covenant between Me and You'" (Gen. 17:9-11).

This indelible mark of Jewish identification with the Covenant has succeeded in distinguishing the Jewish people from the other nations. As is well known, the Nazis used this mark of distinction in identifying Jewish males during the Holocaust. It was therefore necessary for Dr. Freud to flee Vienna when the Nazis invaded Austria. It is significant to note that this ancient Biblical Covenant with Abraham is still very much operative today in defining Jewish identity.

In therapy, the issue of maintaining one's identity is intricately related to one's feelings about self. This is so important especially when the patient is pressured to please others rather than oneself, becoming an "as if" person, instead of being true to oneself. Apparently, Moses recognized that this human tendency to "follow the crowd" would lead Israel astray from its special identity of being partners and committed to keeping the Covenant with G-d and to the Torah.

Researchers in social sciences have shown that it is often the insecure individual who abandons his roots in order to assimilate into the greater dominant society. This frequently turns out to be an illusion, because the alienation experienced in the dominant society today is greater than ever. We live in larger buildings where people have little personal interaction with each other. Contact through e-mail and computers serve as poor substitutes for human connectedness. Families also struggle with greater financial burdens and time constraints, further limiting inter-family communication.

These conditions lead the alienated to seek out other cultures in order to form an identity and feeling of belonging instead of locking into one's own. Assimilation, therefore, compounds the problem rather than offering a viable solution.

Moses, thousands of years ago, addresses this issue by highlighting the dangers of assimilation into the decadent Canaanite culture. He correctly targets the underlying issues to be forging a strong sense of identity in the people that is separate and different from that of the surrounding nations. The foundation for their new identity lies in fulfilling the mandate contained in their covenantal relationship with G-d. The specifics in following this mandate are spelled out in the Torah structure, laid out meticulously by Moses during his lifetime.

Remarkably, Moses' prescription for forging this identity is very much in line with Erikson's developmental stages. It is anchored in the importance of the family structure in instilling a sense of self and identification with a strong set of group values. His admonishment of the people centers on the psychological problem of their inability to internalize his message. Have they developed a comfort level with their new-found sense of separate identity to persevere in the face of foreign influences and differences? Will these adolescent children forever need an external police figure to keep them in line? He is very prescient to the ever-present problem and temptation of assimilation, and admonishes them accordingly.

The warning that Moses gives the people is akin to the talks parents have with their children when they go off to college and experience their first real separation. Parents remind their children that they will no longer be present to police their activities. This separation marks the end of adolescence and the beginning of the next developmental stage of adulthood. This implies assuming responsibility for their actions, loyalty to family and group values and the formation of a strong inner identity. As Moses' physical presence is about to end, his extended family will be sorely challenged to demonstrate the effectiveness of his teachings.

Ha'azinu
Deuteronomy 32:1-32:52
Moses' Closing Hymn

*T*his Parshah opens with Moses composing a Farewell Song
in majestic prose alluded to in the previous Parshah. He
addresses heaven and earth to become witnesses to the Divine
truths he is about to utter. G-d is depicted as the righteous Father
who is spurned by His wayward children. History attests to G-d's
caring concern for His children, especially in the wilderness,
and is repaid by their ingratitude and rebelliousness. Their
actions provoke G-d's anger resulting in distancing Himself
from them and inviting all kinds of retribution. The only
mitigating factor is G-d's recognition of the excessive taunt and
sinfulness of the surrounding heathen nations. Moses concludes
his impassioned song with words of consolation to Israel and
promising retribution to its enemies. Moses is then instructed
to ascend Mt. Nebo, take a last look at the Promised Land and
be prepared to be "gathered unto his people."

The First Psychoanalysis

When patients come into my office to discuss the possibility of treatment, the choice is between psychotherapy and psychoanalysis. In general, psychotherapy is more issue oriented, trying to solve a particular crisis or problem with various explorations of "how to."

Psychoanalysis is a deeper, more intrusive, complicated journey that requires free association, intensive reflection, searching and connecting the past with the present. In this process, the patient begins to experience and understand how family history, inner fantasies, past behavior and unconscious processes interface with one another, enabling the analyst to then produce a more informed position for choice and change. In order to do this effectively, the analyst must first provide the conditions for safety. This safety is formed by a series of boundaries which allow for secure and safe exploration, e.g., complete confidentiality, whereas the analyst maintains neutrality by not revealing himself/herself.

In this week's *Parshah*, *Ha'azinu* (Listen), G-d sets up the provisions of safety by providing clear boundaries for the Israelites about how to keep themselves separate, pure and safe. Moses then begins his own psychoanalysis, as it were, in poetic form, by reviewing his role in the past history of his extended Israelite family up to this point. He is also acting as their analyst by interpreting where they came from, what they experienced and how that impacted their lives.

Moses begins their analysis as follows, "Remember the days of old, consider the years of many generations; ask thy father and he will declare it unto thee. Thine elders and they will tell thee" (Deut. 32:7). This retrospective exploration is the beginning of a poetic reflective search into their unique identity, who were their ancestors, and a review of their trials and tribulations that brought them to where they are today. Moses' interpretation of this search is to remind them that not only are they a product of their ancestry, but that they must remember they are a covenanted people with G-d which constitutes a collaborative partnership. The condition of safety applies, which means that the boundaries must be observed, otherwise the partnership becomes void. When violations occur, much work must be done to reset the boundaries and to find out where they were violated in order to continue their journey safely in the analysis.

G-d, the Supreme Analyst, as it were, not only interprets their breaking of the boundaries of safety together with their consequences, but is able to verbalize the unconscious wishes and desires that lie hidden in the psyche of the Israelites. They wish to consort with other gods and be unfaithful. They wish for vengeance and do the forbidden. G-d realizes that revealing these unconscious wishes is necessary because if they are not aware of these hidden forbidden desires, they cannot make the effort to control them and they will suffer dire consequences.

The analysis ends with Moses warning the people "Set your heart unto all the words wherewith I testify against you this day; that ye may charge your children therewith to observe to do all the words of this law...because it is your life, and through this thing ye shall prolong your days upon the land, whither ye go over the Jordan to possess it" (Deut. 32:46-47).

Zot Ha-Berachah
Deuteronomy 33:1-34:12
Moses' Farewell Blessing

In this concluding Parshah in Devarim, the fifth and last book of the Torah, Moses proceeds to bless each of the twelve tribes of Israel prior to his death. Speaking again in majestic prose, Moses introduces his blessing by referring to the revelation at Sinai as the seminal moment in establishing their identity as a nation. In blessing each of the tribes, he lavishes special praise upon his native tribe of Levi, who remained loyal to G-d in the wilderness, and were the guardians of the Sanctuary and all its vessels. The last chapter describes in moving detail, Moses' ascent of Mt. Nebo, his surveying all of the Promised Land, and his being buried in an unknown unmarked grave. In a prophetic postscript, the Torah declares, "And there hath not risen a prophet since in Israel like unto Moses, whom the Lord knew face to face" (Deut. 34:10).

The Uniqueness of Moses: Prophet-Analyst

As we begin the last *Parshah*, *Zot Ha-Berachah* (This is the Blessing) in Deuteronomy, the last of the Five Books of Moses, we also come to the end of Moses' life and tenure as leader and architect of the new nation, Israel. His uniqueness is attested to by the Torah in its final assessment of him, "And there hath not risen a prophet in Israel like unto Moses, whom the Lord knew face to face…" (Deut. 34:10). This rare testimonial is the Torah's way of further emphasizing the uniqueness of each individual. This quality of uniqueness is extended to include each of the twelve tribes, as Moses proceeds to bless them in his poetic style as introduced in the previous *Parshah*. His blessing is geared to the unique talents and abilities of each tribe, in order to encourage them to fulfill their respective roles in the land of Israel.

In administering his final blessings to each of the tribes, Moses is following the example of the patriarch Jacob/Israel in blessing his twelve sons before his death. Jacob, whom we might call the first "vocational counselor," was able to adapt his projections of his sons' future vocations according to their individual abilities and characteristics. Moses does this now on a collective scale, based on their signature characteristics, and on the caliber of leadership within each tribe.

For example, in blessing his tribe of Levi, Moses says, "For they have observed Thy word, and keep Thy Covenant. They shall teach Jacob Thy ordinances, and Israel Thy law; they shall put incense before Thee and whole burnt offerings upon Thine altar"

251

(Deut. 33:9-10). Moses recognizes the characteristic of extreme loyalty of his kindred tribe in the face of the rebelliousness of other tribes, by forecasting their role as religious leaders and teachers in future generations.

The character transformation of Moses, which is a part of his uniqueness, is symbolic of the psychological development embarked upon by the Children of Israel. Moses' life began with the trauma of temporary separation from his family, which had a great bearing on his subsequent emotional development, especially his volatile temper and anger (killing the Egyptian, breaking the commandments, striking the rock) which ultimately prevented him from completing his mission of entering the Promised Land. However, in our discussions on the weekly Torah readings we have seen his remarkable character development, his willingness to give up his life and future in order to save his people, his ability to listen and implement the judicial system recommended by his father-in-law Jethro, his overseeing the building of the Mishkan, his being the intermediary in transmitting the Torah on Mt. Sinai and his extraordinary patience and suffering induced by a rebellious stiff-necked people, all encompass attributes of character that are truly extraordinary.

The Torah alludes to this progression of character development in the nomenclature by which Moses is addressed during the course of his career. As a young refugee shepherd living in Midian, he is referred to by his future wife, Zipporah, as *ish mitzri* (an Egyptian), "An Egyptian delivered us out of the hands of the shepherds" (Exod. 2:19). At this early stage in his career, Moses' external Egyptian identity clashes with his Hebraic roots, reflecting a conflicted inner identity. Evidence of the consolidation of Moses' identity into that of a "man" owning a secure ego and no longer identified as an Egyptian, occurs when he announces the coming of the last of the ten plagues.

At this stage the Torah declares, "*Ish*, the man Moses was very great in the land of Egypt in the sight of Pharaoh's servants and in the sight of the people" (Exod. 11:3). The identity of

Moses as an Israelite is clearly acknowledged by all Egyptians. His deeper spiritual self and unique intimate connection with G-d is later attested to when he is vindicated from the personal attacks by his older siblings, Miriam and Aaron. At that point the Torah states, "*Avdi* [my servant] Moses, in my house, he is most trusted." (Num. 12:7).

At the end of his career, the Torah accords him the highest tribute as his identity now becomes *ish ha-Elokim*, man of G-d. (Deut. 33:1) Upon Moses' death, this later designation is reinforced as the Torah refers to him simply as *eved YHWH*, servant of G-d (Deut. 34:5). Moses' relationship with G-d has become internalized and has evolved to the point where his identity is one of total commitment to doing G-d's will. In tracking these references, we see the Torah's psychological insights into the unfolding character transformation of Moses from being an Egyptian to that of being a man of G-d. His life personifies the message he brings to his people, which is not only the conquest of the external enemies, but the internal enemies as well.

The miraculous transformation of this "rag tag" assemblage of Egyptian slaves into an aspiring *am kadosh*—a holy nation, in a period of forty years in the wilderness, serves as a fitting sequel to the character transformation of their mentor, Moses. The forty years of wandering in the wilderness turns out to be a necessary therapeutic period in the Israelites' psychological makeup, which has its roots in the patriarchal period. Beginning with the patriarchs as the founding role models, the Israelites acquire a separate identity and morph into an independent nation governed by the Torah, with a judicial system to implement it. They are struggling with this separate identity in the face of the allure of surrounding nations immersed in idolatry and immorality. G-d, the Supreme Analyst, as it were, is aware of the hidden evil unconscious desires of His subjects, who are drawn to these surrounding temptations, yet shows infinite patience after administering the necessary discipline and structure that a parent must provide for the benefit of His errant children. This Torah structure includes the basic conditions for growth and development such as safety, nurture, boundaries, decision-making, morality and goal-setting. The real test of the degree to which they have internalized this structure will come later, after the conquest when the Israelites and the conquered nations are living together.

In these weekly Torah readings, we have not only a record of events and narratives, but character studies of various personalities when viewed from the lens of psychological insight. We have seen the internal development of the Israelites, from their infantile need for immediate gratification to being able to stand patiently at Mt. Sinai and declare, *na'aseh ve-nishma*, "We will do and we will hearken." We have seen their development from childish narcissism to the recognition of concern for others as stated, *ve-ahavta le-reiacha ka-mocha*, "Love thy neighbor as thyself." We have seen their gradual development from chaotic self-centered behavior to more disciplined structured morality. The Israelites have marched forward to their external physical goal of the Promised Land, but in tandem, have moved forward in their internal development toward the goal of greater maturity as a holy nation.

It is no wonder that out of this advanced psychologically perceptive heritage emerged Dr. Sigmund Freud, founder of the discipline known today as psychoanalysis. It is this discipline which has helped me illuminate the inner emotional and psychological path taken by the Israelites in their development toward maturity as a people. It is also another convincing reason why the Torah has remained the most influential book ever written.

About the Author

Dr. Vivian Skolnick received her doctorate in psychology at the Illinois Institute of Technology and is a registered clinical psychologist. She is a graduate of the Chicago Center for Psychoanalysis, where she is a faculty member. She is an affiliate member of the Society of the Chicago Institute for Psychoanalysis and Membership Chairperson of Nefesh International. Dr. Skolnick has published in professional journals and presented papers on topics related to psychology and religion. She resides in Chicago where she is in private practice as a clinical psychologist and psychoanalyst providing both treatment and supervision. Dr. Skolnick is married, has two married children and nine grandchildren.

BIBLIOGRAPHY

Alexander, F. (1950). *Psychosomatic Medicine*. New York: Norton.

Andrews, E. (1974). *The Emotionally Disturbed Family*. New York: J. Aronson.

Arieti, S. (1976). *Creativity: The Magic Synthesis*. New York: Basic Books Inc.

Beit-Halami, B; Argyle, M. (1975). "God as Father-Protection: The Theory and Evidence." *British Journal of Medical Psychology*, 48.

Bergler, E. (1953). *Fashion and the Unconscious*. New York: International Universities Press.

Blos, P. (1962). *On Adolescence: A Psychoanalytic Interpretation*. New York: The Free Press.

Bollas, C. (1997). "Attachment." *The Attachment and Loss Trilogy*. (Vol. 1). London: Pimlico.

Bollas, C. (1987). *The Shadow of the Object: Psychoanalysis of the Unthought Known*. New York: Columbia University Press.

Boris, H. (1994). *Envy*. Northvale, N.J.: Aronson.

Brenner, C. (1973). *An Elementary Textbook of Psychoanalysis*. Rev. Ed. New York: Anchor Books.

Bucci, W. (2001). "Pathways of Emotional Communication." *Psychoanalytic Inquiry*, 21, 40.

Coen, S. J. (1992). *The Misuse of Persons: Analyzing Pathological Dependency*. Hillsdale, NJ: Analytic Press.

Dosick, Rabbi W. (1995). *Living Judaism: The Complete Guide to Jewish Belief, Tradition and Practice*. San Francisco: HarperSanFrancisco.

Emmons, R. A., McCullough, M. E. (2004). *The Psychology of Gratitude*. New York: Oxford University Press.

Erikson, E. H. (1982). *Identity and Religion*. New York: Seabury Press.

Fainberg, H. (2005). *The Telescoping of Generations: Listening to the Narcissistic Links Between Generations.* London and New York: Routledge.

Finell, Schumacher, J. eds. (1997). *Mind-Body Problems: Psychotherapy with Psychosomatic Disorders.* Northvale, NJ: Jason Aronson.

Fowler, J. (1995). *Stages of Faith: The Psychology of Human Development.* San Francisco: HarperOne.

Freud, S. (1989). J. Strachey (Ed. & Trans.). *The Standard Edition of the Complete Psychological Works of Sigmund Freud.* New York: W.W. Norton.

Freud, S. (1989). *The Interpretation of Dreams.* In J. Strachey (Ed. & Trans.). *The Standard Edition of the Complete Psychological Works of Sigmund Freud.* (Vols. 4 and 5). New York: W.W. Norton.

Freud, S. (1989). *Group Psychology and the Analysis of the Ego.* In J. Strachey (Ed. & Trans.). *The Standard Edition of the Complete Psychological Works of Sigmund Freud.* (Vol. 18). New York: W.W. Norton.

Freud, S. (1989). On *Narcissism: An Introduction.* In J. Strachey (Ed. & Trans.). *The Standard Edition of the Complete Psychological Works of Sigmund Freud.* (Vol. 14). New York: W.W. Norton.

Fromm, E. (1950). *Psychoanalysis and Religion.* Binghamton, New York: Vail-Ballou Press.

Fromm, E. (1956). *The Art of Loving,* Binghamton, New York: Harper Collins Publishers.

Greenberg, D., Witztum, E. (1949). *Sanity and Sanctity: Mental Health Work Among the Ultra-Orthodox Jews.* New Haven and New York: Yale University Press.

Grinker, R.R. (1973). *Psychosomatic Concepts,* rev. ed. New York: J. Aronson.

Grinstein, A. (1983). *Freud's Rules of Dream Interpretation.* New York, N.Y.: International Universities Press.

Hafen, B. Q. and et al. (1996). *Mind/body Health: The Effects of Attitudes, Emotions, and Relationships.* Boston: Allyn and Bacon.

Hertz, J.H. (1980). *The Pentateuch and Haftorahs*. London: Soncino Press.

Kamenetzky, Rabbi M. *Weekly Parshah Summary* (Fax-Homily Series), New York.

Kavaler-Adler, S. (2003). *Mourning, Spirituality, and Psychic Change: A New Object Relations View of Psychoanalysis*. Hove, East Sussex. Reprint, New York: Routledge, Brunner.

Klein, M. (1988). *Envy and Gratitude*. London: Virago Press Ltd.

Kohut, H. (1971). *The Analysis of Self*. New York: International Universities Press.

Meissner, W.W. (2008). "The Role of Language in the Development of the Self III: The Significance of the Pronouns." *Psychoanalytic psychology*, 25, 242-246.

Milne, A. A. (1961, © 1927). *Now We Are Six*. New York: Dutton.

Natterson, J. M., ed. (1980). *The Dream in Clinical Practice: Classical Psycho-Analysis and its Applications*. New York: J. Aronson.

Ostow, M., Scharfstein, B. (1960). *The Need to Believe: The Psychology of Religion*. New York: Universities Press, Inc.

Pirkei Avot (*Ethics of the fathers*). (1949), In P. Birnbaum (Ed. & Trans.). New York: Hebrew Publishing Company.

Reik, T. (1948). *Listening with the Third Ear*. New York. Pyramid Books.

Rizzuto, A. (1979). *The Birth of the Living God*. Chicago and London: University of Chicago Press.

Rothstein, A. (1984). *The Narcissistic Pursuit of Perfection*, 2nd rev. ed. New York: International Universities Press.

Ryan, R. M, and Deci, E. L. (February 2001). "On Happiness and Human Potential." *Annual Review of Psychology*. 52, 166.

Ryan, R; Kasser, and Timand. (1993). "A Dark Side to the American Dream: Correlates of Financial Success as a Central Life Aspiration." *Journal of Personality and Social Psychology*.

Schafer, R. (1983). *The Analytic Attitude*. London: Hogarth.

Sheldon, K.M., and Kasser, T.. (1998). "Pursuing Personal Goals: Skills Enable Progress but not all Progress is Beneficial." *Personality and Psychological Bulletin* 24, 1319-1331.

Sheldon, K.M., Ryan, R.M., Deci, E.L., and Kasser, T.. (2004). "Independent Effects of Goal Contents and Motives on Well-Being: It's Both What You Pursue and Why You Pursue it." *Personality and Psychological Bulletin* 30, 475-486.

Sherman, S., Lanham, D.S. (2006). ed. Hushion. *Understanding Adoption: Clinical Work with Adults, Parents and Children.* New York. J. Aronson.

Soloveitchick, Rabbi J.B. (1974). "The Halacha of the First Day." In J. Reimer (Ed.) *Jewish Reflections on Death.* New York: Schocken Books

Sperling, M. (1985). *Psychosomatic Disorders in Childhood.* New York: Jason Aronson.

Vargas, P. T., Yoon, S. (2006). "On the Psychology of Materialism: Wanting Things, Having Things, and Being Happy." *Advertising & Society Review* 7, no. 1 (2006).

Winnicott, D.W. (1958). "Transitional Objects and Transitional Phenomena." In *Collected Papers: Through Paediatrics to Psychoanalysis.* London: Tavistock Publications.

Wishnie, H. (1977). *The Impulsive Personality: Understanding People with Destructive Character Disorders.* New York: Plenum Press.

Zeligs, D. F. (1988). *Psychoanalysis and the Bible: A Study in Depth of Seven Leaders.* New York: Human Sciences Press.

GLOSSARY

The Glossary below is not meant to be comprehensive. However, it covers the majority of Hebrew terms found in this work

Akeidah: (Lit., binding) Popularly translated as "sacrifice" (of Isaac).

Am: Nation or People,

Amcha: Derivative of Am, denoting "rank and file" of the people.

Ashkenaz: Originally of "German" Jewish ancestry, but now refers broadly to "East European" Jewry; (adj.) *Ashkenazi*, (pl.) *Ashkenazim*.

Avodah: In Biblical Hebrew refers to priestly "service" in the sanctuary.

Bereshith: "Genesis," the first book in the Torah.

Brit/Brith: "Covenant" also refers to circumcision, when an eight day old male child enters the Covenant of Israel.

Drash: "Inquiry," same root as Midrash. The scholarly art of Biblical interpretation also known as hermeneutics or exegesis.

Gemara: Rabbinical debates and discussions based on the Mishnah.

Hacham: Wise person.

Hachnasat Orhim: (Lit., welcoming guests) Hospitality.

Halachah: (Lit. going/guidance)Legal decision of the Rabbis.

Halom: Dream.

Hametz: Leavening. Foods containing leavening are forbidden during Passover.

Hatan: Groom.

Humra: Restriction. Strict interpretation of the law; (pl.) *humrot*.

Im: If.

Ish: Man.

Kadosh: Holy (adj).

Kedushah: Holiness (noun).

Kiddush Hashem: Sanctification of G-d's name.

Kohen: Priest; a descendant of the first high priest Aaron from the tribe of Levi.

Korban: Sacrifice; (pl.) *korbanot.*

Kvetching: Yiddish for complaining or griping.

Lashon: (Lit., *tongue*) Language.

Lashon hara: Evil talk.

Luhot: Tablets; the Ten Commandments which were inscribed on two stone tablets.

Malach: Angel; (pl.) *malachim.*

Mehitzah: Partition. In modern usage refers to the divider between the sexes at religious services-- ----

Menorah: The seven-branched Candelabrum in the Mishkan.

Metzora: One who is afflicted with a serious "skin disease" (*tzaraat)* commonly referred to as leprosy.

Midrash: (Lit., inquiry): A large collection of Rabbinical interpretations, stories, folklore, legends and homilies (sermonic teachings) about the Bible. It was compiled from approximately 500 BCE. until the mid–1500's CE. It is divided into *Midrash Halachah* (legal) based on Jewish law and *Midrash Aggadah*, legends and lore; (pl) *midrashim.*

Mishkan: Portable "Tabernacle" existed during the early Biblical period, later replaced by the Temple in Jerusalem.

Mishnah: (Lit., learn, repeat): "Law code" compiled by Rabbi Judah the Prince in 200 CE. Foundation of the Oral Law. Later together with the *Gemara* (see above) became known as the Talmud.

Mitzvah: (Lit., commandment): In modern usage a "good deed." There are 613 commandments in the Torah: 248 positive "Thou Shalt" and 365 prohibitions "Thou shalt not."

Mizbeach: Altar upon which the various sacrifices were offered.

Moshe: Hebrew/Egyptian name for "Moses."

Mum: "Defect" or physical liability. Pertains to humans as well as to animals; (pl.) *mumim*.

Musar: Exhortation.

Ner Tamid: "Eternal Light," symbolized today by a lamp in the synagogue over the Holy Ark.

Nisan: First month of the Jewish lunar calendar corresponding to the month of April.

Olah: (Lit. goes up [in smoke]): Burnt offering; one of the many types of sacrifices in the *Mishkan*, which was completely burned.

Parshah: "Portion" of the Torah read sequentially at Sabbath services over the course of a year beginning with Genesis and concluding with Deuteronomy. *Parshat* is the construct form of *Parshah* meaning, "portion of"; (pl.) *Parshiyot*.

Phylacteries: See *Tefillin* below.

Pidyon ha-ben: "Redemption of the firstborn son," which occurs at the end of the infant's first month. The redemption consists of the father giving five (5) silver shekels (dollars) to a *Kohen* who is G-d's representative in the ceremony.

Pirkei Avot: (Lit., *Chapters of the Fathers*) Best known book in the Mishnah, is a collection of wise ethical sayings and maxims of the Rabbis spanning many hundreds of years.

Rashi: Foremost commentator on the Bible and Talmud. Rashi is an acronym taken from the initials of his name, *Rav* (Rabbi) *Shlomo* (Solomon) *ben* (son of) *Yitzchak* (Isaac). He lived in France (1040-1105).

Sanhedrin: "Supreme Court" of seventy-one jurists. It is estimated that the *Sanhedrin* functioned intermittently from the time of Moses to approximately 500 CE.

Sephard: Jews of Spanish ancestry who emigrated to Greece, Turkey, North Africa and the Middle East; (adj.) *Sephardi*; (pl.) *Sephardim*.

Shalom: "Peace." Also used in modern Hebrew for "hello" and "goodbye."

Shema: "ear." A reference to the declaration of faith as written in Deut. 6:4.

Shemot: (Lit., names): "Exodus," the second book in the Torah.

Shofar: Ram's horn traditionally blown on Rosh Hashanah. In Biblical times used to announce important events.

Siman: Sign, omen.

Sukkot: Booths in which the Israelites lived during their sojourn in the wilderness after the exodus from Egypt.

Talmud: (Lit., study): The sixty-volume Babylonian collection of the Oral Law consisting of the *Mishnah* and *Gemara* (see above). The Jerusalem edition of the Talmud is much smaller and less authoritative. The Talmud is the recognized source for all Jewish law.

Tam: Whole, complete.

Tefillin: Phylacteries; small black boxes containing passages of the Torah worn at morning weekday services. Based on Deut. 6:8.

Terumah: (Lit., elevating) Donation, usually associated with gifts to the priests.

Teshuvah: Repentance.

Tikkun Olam: (Lit., repairing the world): One of the goals of Judaism.

Tochachah: Admonishment, curse.

Torah: (Lit., instruction): Originally associated with the five (5) Books of Moses, but used loosely today to encompass the Bible as well as the entire body of Rabbinic literature.

Tzaraat: A serious skin disease, usually associated with leprosy.

Tzitzit: Fringes worn on the four (4) corners of a garment. See Num. 15:38.

Yiddish: (Lit. Jewish): The vernacular spoken by East European Jews.

Yisrael: Hebrew for "Israel."

Zechut: Merit or protecting influence, frequently linked with the *Avot* (Patriarchs).